AF415338

#52

---

*A **52-WEEK** JOURNEY OF INSPIRING
LESSONS
TO UPLIFT AND EMPOWER
YOUNG MEN OF COLOR*

Table Of Contents

1ST QUARTER - DISCOVERY

2ND QUARTER - LEARNING & BALANCE

By: Damar Christopher

Sr. Director, Product Management

By: Bryan Henriquez

Entrepreneur

By: Dante Seay

Engineer, Entrepreneur

4TH QUARTER - REACHING YOUR GOALS

By: Dr. Kevin D. Williams

Minister

By: Mark Kim

Finance

By: Devin Christopher

Co-Working/Community Manager

By: Otis Idlebird

Entrepreneur

Greetings from the Editor-To my young brotha's of color.

The year 2020 was one of the most emotionally charged years I have ever seen. There were riots, police shootings, knees on necks, and a bold display of racial injustice. Streets were filled with people no longer accepting the status quo and marching against it. Black Lives Matter, Antifa, and Proud Boys provoked even more tension and divide in our country. Jobs were lost, and people were losing their livelihood, homes, medical benefits, and going without food. Children had to stay home and attend school virtually, while many parents had to balance homeschooling, and making ends meet with less money. Pressure was building daily. In addition to everything else happening, we also had to contend with the pandemic and the global shutdown caused by Covid-19.

The shutdown had us scrambling for bottled water, toilet paper, paper towels, and canned food. The grocery stores could not stock the shelves fast enough. People were afraid, and rightfully so. Most of us have never experienced anything like this before. We could not have even imagined this happening in our lifetime.

2020 was a year to remember!

It sparked the creation of this book. I personally know a lot of young men currently without fathers in the home. Single Motherhood and incarcerations are on the rise. Young men are amid massive chaos, turmoil, hatred, and racism. You fight battles that are seen and hidden inward. Which direction should you go? Who should you turn to for help? How long must you sit and wait before acting? Many young men are misguided and sent in directions not conducive to either their health, wealth, or overall wellbeing. Having gone through so much already, and still going through it at the time of this writing, you can be better prepared in how you deal and respond to these challenges.

 I along with some others want to provide you with a roadmap as a resource to navigate you through the peaks and valleys of life. We want you to have answers to your questions. These answers will give you a variety of options from positive perspectives. These answers are in a format that is not only accessible, but entertaining while promoting growth and development. This is a 52-week book covering different topics along with a CALL TO ACTION for each week. The writings will empower you to embrace who you are and grow into the leaders you were meant to be.

This book contains the collaboration of over 40 strong men of color. These men agreed to lend a hand to offer support and guidance to build you up. You will read different styles of writing. The backgrounds of these men vary, the vocations are diverse, but the intent is unified.

Read a story each week and apply the CALL TO ACTION at the end of each story. Track your growth over the course of 52 weeks, you will be glad you did. We love you and we want to see you successful in all aspects of life. Do your thing!

Ernie D. Seay, Editor

1ST QUARTER

DISCOVERY

BREAKING THE CHAINS (PSALMS 107:14)

By: Autavius Hobbs

Pharmacy Account Manager

Objective – To understand that God is powerful enough to break all the chains in your life that have prevented you from having a physical, mental, and spiritual breakthrough.

The phrase "Breaking the Chains" is often used to describe when an individual breaks away from a problematic pattern or behavior. This phrase can be applied to all aspects of life. When we carefully examine ourselves, we begin to identify the chains in our lives that hold us back from reaching our optimal level. A chain is something that binds or restrains an object or individual. They are often used to restrict the freedom of a human or animal. However, chains can also be used to create a bond which symbolizes interconnectivity and interdependence. These descriptions help us to understand that chains are necessary when used appropriately. The chains that we will discuss are chains used to restrict our liberty and our freedom. These are the chains that need to be broken in our lives.

In Psalms 107:14 (NIV), the Bible says, *"He brought them out of darkness, the utter darkness, and broke away their chains."* Let me start off by stating that the "He" referred to in the verse is "God". God represents the source of deliverance all through Psalms Chapter 107. If you take time to read this chapter, you will see a series of people being delivered from the chains in life that kept them from being happy and successful. For the next few minutes, let's take a few moments and talk about some of the chains that often hold us back in life.

Some of us struggle with Chains **of Self-Consciousness**. This chain binds us to a worrisome and unhealthy fixation on what others might think of you. As we enter our teenage years, it may feel like we are under a microscope. Our friends notice every pimple on our face, the name brands on our clothes. They also often make fun of us for being either too short, tall, fat, or skinny. It seems like every day we must wake up and prove ourselves to others so that we can win their vote of confidence. Over time this creates a chain of self-consciousness. We allow others to hold us back from being who we want to be because deep down inside we want their approval. Sometimes we even go to the extreme just to fit in. I know young people who get their hair cut a certain way, put tattoos on their body and get multiple body piercings. Some also steal from others just so that they can buy name brand clothes and shoes for the sake of acceptance. If you or anyone you know needs someone to break this chain, I know the right person to call. In Psalms 139:14 (NIV), the Bible says, "I praise you because *I am fearfully and wonderfully made.*" This verse speaks directly to each one of us. God made us all in a unique way and we should not let anyone attach a chain to us that makes us feel bad about how who we are or how we may look. We are all beautiful in God's sight because He made us in His image. If you are struggling to get free from the chains of being Self-Conscious, allow God to break this chain for you today, so that you can be free to be you.

Some of us struggle with the **Chains of Racism.** Racism is hatred or intolerance of another race or other races. Racism influences the mistreatment of others. As a result of this mistreatment, some people develop bad emotions and feelings of inferiority. Individuals who are considered minorities often struggle with the effects of racism throughout their lives. They grow up with the belief that they are inferior to others because of the color of their skin. As they get older, they begin to see differences in how they are treated when they are away from their homes. Minorities are often segregated to certain neighborhoods and schools. In addition to this, some minorities grow up with negative feelings toward police officers because, they see many minorities being shot each year due to police brutality. The truth is no one is considered a second-class citizen in the eyes of God. In Galatians 3:26-29, the Bible helps us to understand that all of God's children are one big family. He helps break this mental chain of racism that we grow up with by removing the labels and boxes that society tries to define and place others in. Imagine a world in which we can think freely about ourselves without looking down on others, or have others look down on us, because of the family that we were born in. If you are struggling to get free from the chains of racism, allow

God to break this chain for you today so that you can set your mind free.

Finally, some of us struggle with the **Chains of Sin**. This could be described as a spiritual chain. Sin can be described as a transgression against God. When we sin, we are missing the mark. When we look at the people God helped in Psalms 107, we can see that some of those individuals put themselves in bad positions because they were not obedient. One thing that we must learn is that obedience is a key that will open many doors for you in this life. Some people think it is uncool to be obedient to their parents, teachers, and even police officers. However, each time we practice disobedience we fall deeper into the pool of sin. I am glad that God is a God of mercy and a God that gives us second chances in life. We need to look to Him to help us break away from these chains of sin that have trapped all of us at one point or another. God sent His son Jesus to die so that all of us would have an opportunity to be saved. We can become a child of God by hearing his word, believing his word, and repenting our sins. Repenting of our sins means that we decide to change our lives and confess to him. Then we are baptized, which washes our sins away. If you are struggling to get free from the chains of sin, allow God to break this chain for you today so that you may one day live with him eternally.

CALL TO ACTION:

1. Think about one thing about yourself that makes you "unique/special" (i.e., smile, personality, attitude). This is what helps you bless the lives of others despite how you look physically. Embrace this all week.

2. Think about a person or group of people that recently mistreated you or someone you know. Send up a prayer for them asking that God give them a change of heart.

3. Read Psalms 139 each day to remind yourself of how special you are to God and to see a glimpse of His Power.

As you continue your journey in this life, always remember that you should not let anyone, or anything hold you back. You will find yourself caught in different kinds of chains from to time, but if you know God, all your chains can be broken. Now that you have been introduced to the one who can break the chains, share this lesson with your friends. Help them to discover that they do not have to live life feeling like they are restricted or inferior. When you and your friends are set free from these chains, you will see life through a different lens which will allow you to be successful and break down doors that once seemed unmovable. God bless you.

NOTES

STAY TRUE

By: Kevin Wilson

Manager – Frito Lay

I challenge each young man to stay true to himself. Never forget your roots, the core, the soil, and foundation in which you were brought up in. Proverbs 22:6, "Train up a child in the way he should go, and when he is old, he will not depart from it." As each of you keep true to your upbringing, take the road less traveled.

Value yourself, know your worth, continue to educate yourself. Never allow anyone to define you as a man. Strive to be the best at whatever you set your mind to. Haters will come, haters will go, times are unstable and unfair, but only you and God know how far you will go. "Walk by faith, not by sight." 2 Corinthians 5:7

CALL TO ACTION:

As you build yourself, grow your wealth. Invest in your financial future by:

1. Participate in your company's match 401k plan.

2. Learn to live off 80 percent of your take home pay. Why 80 percent? Because the Lord will not leave you broke.

   2a. Give 10 percent back to the Lord or benevolence. (I have been young, and now am old, yet I have not seen the righteous forsaken or his children begging for bread.) Psalm 37:25

   2b. Save 10 percent for yourself (Don't spend every dime you make) Remember Proverbs 22:7 "The rich rules over the poor, And the borrower becomes the lender's slave."

The LORD is my light and my salvation; Whom shall I fear? The LORD is the strength of my life; Of whom shall I be afraid? Psalms 27:1

NOTES

CAN'T HAVE EVERYTHING

By: Collin Christopher

Sales Development Representative

All my life I've resented the idea that a person can't have everything. You've probably heard this sentiment echoed about as many times as I have. "You can't have it all," people have said meaning well, but frustrating me to no end. I felt like that was such a defeatist attitude. I also wondered if white children heard this "advice" as much as black children do. Regardless of our socioeconomic background, black people are taught to temper their expectations and be realistic about what we want, about the goals we set, and ultimately about the world which we build for ourselves and those around us. This leads to futures devoid of imagination. We tell ourselves that certain objects in our lives are immovable, until someone else with more resources, or simply more support, comes along and moves that object. As we watch them do that, we watch our lives go by without taking risks big enough to change our realities.

The only person in my life who never told me that I couldn't have it all was my father. Because of him I believe I can. I've cherished his words because of how earnest they were, and how much they challenged me and continue to force me to push my limits. "You know what, you actually can have it all," he said, as if he'd just realized it for himself. "You just have to be willing to work for it." The concept of earning it, doing the dirty work, day in and day out until you wring the proper results out of the stubborn hands of life, inspired me throughout high school and college. There are two central reasons I strived for this in my life. First, I wanted to be able to look back on my life and not have any regrets about the things I could have done if I were more determined. Determination is a sign of strength, and as a man, I tend to define myself by strength in many areas. There are only a few things that are extremely hard for me to live with, and regret is one of them. Yes, you can regret doing something, but you can also regret not doing things that you deeply wish you would have. I've looked into the eyes of many men much older than me and saw their regret of not doing. It eats at them into their twilight years. I have since tried to escape being food for my own indecision. The second reason was my desire to prove to everyone who told me that I couldn't have everything, that I could. Most likely by the time I realized this goal, they probably wouldn't care at that point.

You may be wondering, what does "everything" look like? To me, it's physical health, and a strong and open relationship with my family. It also includes a good amount of trustworthy and bright friends who are successful and push me to be successful. Lastly, financial stability, wealth, an occupation that is fulfilling, and reciprocated love with a significant other. For you, it may be these things, or a different set of goals. Either way, I want to challenge you to set goals that will make people think, "Isn't that a bit too much to ask for? This sounds like a perfect life, and no one is perfect, so how do you expect to have all of this?"

These are valid questions, but honestly the answer is very simple, flexibility. I have failed at plenty of things in life, which means I haven't succeeded in getting everything I ever wanted. Life will humble you over and over, but if I've learned one thing so far, it is that you must learn how to bend without breaking. My mother will tell you that one of my favorite things I use to say as a child when something went wrong was, "It's ok!" No matter what happened, I figured then as I do now, that positivity and reframing the situation is a matter of choice. We can change our expectations and our desires at any time. We can work through the circumstances handed to us, but we don't change them directly, we only handle them as they are.

That isn't to say that you just blindly accept whatever happens to you in life, whether it be success or failure. You have to keep moving forward until you realize that you may be pushing in the wrong direction. I used to want very different things, because I had an expectation for how those things "looked" and how they would make me feel. And then I lived a *little*, and I realized I didn't really want what I thought I wanted. I realized the "everything" that my father told me I could have had to be chiseled away at until I reached the core of what was important to me through trial and error.

I think that when most people consider what they want, they're thinking in terms of happiness. Happiness is fleeting, and over time what makes us happy will drastically change, because we will drastically change. I'd like to challenge you to think in terms of contentment. What do you need to be content with your life? In other words, if you suddenly got these things and nothing ever changed, would you be able to live with it? Notice that my list didn't include dollar amounts or arbitrary goals like, "I want to reach this benchmark by the time I'm 30," or so on. Honestly, the list did include that initially, but the concept of contentment changed how I viewed myself and what I wanted out of life. It forced me to come to grips with the difference between what other people told me was important versus what I truly valued. It brought me more happiness because I stopped embracing expectations and desires that weren't ever truly mine to begin with.

CALL TO ACTION:

In case no one has ever told you the truth, I hope you accept it from me. You can have everything! Do yourself a favor though, and don't try to do it all alone. Be content, not satisfied, with wherever you are now, because all you ever have is right now, and the journey to wherever you're going is what defines you. Even if you reach the point where you have everything, never stop challenging yourself to be more and give more.

NOTES

UNREALIZED POTENTIAL

By: Jerry Stephens

Math Specialist at Stafford MSD/Owner Double A+ Tutorials

You miss 100% of the shots that you never take. This has been a very popular statement over the last few years, but what exactly does it mean? It's simple; if you never make any attempts, you don't have any chance for success. As a result of this statement, many people have been encouraged to achieve great success, and have taken chances that they would otherwise have never taken.

HOWEVER, WHAT HAPPENS WHEN YOU TAKE THE SHOT AND YOU MISS?

You finally get the courage to make the attempt and you fail. Now, unlike not taking the shot, everyone now knows that you failed. You are now on public display. You're scrutinized. "How and why did you fail?" You start to think, "Wouldn't it have been better if I hadn't taken the shot?" At least then you can create your own ending of how it would have turned out.

In the 1997 NBA playoffs with 9 seconds left and the score tied, a young player took the final shot, and not only did he miss, he shot an airball. The game went into overtime. Early in overtime he took a second shot and shot a second airball. With 40 seconds left in the round and his team down by 3, he got a chance to tie the score with a 3-pointer and unbelievably he shot *another* air ball. With good team defense his team held and with seven seconds left in the game and his team still down by 3, he got the ball and had a chance to take the last shot. After shooting 3 air balls what do you think happened? Did he pass the ball? Did he take the shot? Did he miss the shot? Stop and think for a moment. After missing 3 embarrassing airballs and the crowd jeering you, what would you do? The fairytale ending would be that he took the shot, made it, sent the game into overtime, and led his team to victory. The reality ending is more dramatic and more exciting than the fairytale ending. In fact, it's more like that of a blockbuster Hollywood movie.

DOUBT (FEAR) KILLS MORE DREAMS THAN FAILURE EVER HAS OR EVER WILL.

Don't doubt or restrict yourself to limitations that others impose upon you, or those that you impose upon yourself. Always look to Christ as your SOURCE and not merely as another resource. Christ has no limitations, and therefore you can do all things through Christ. Understand that fear and faith cannot occupy the same space. Your faith in Christ must be bigger than your doubt in yourself or your fear of failing.

Doubt is the built-in excuse that allows you to take the shot, while you simultaneously think you have no real chance of making it. When you miss, you are ok telling yourself, "I knew I wasn't going to make it anyway," "hey, at least I tried," and many other similar statements. These are the statements caused by doubt that kill dreams and lead to unfulfilled potential.

Have you ever heard of WD-40? You would not have heard of them if they had stopped after their 39th failure. It was on the 40th try they got it right. Hence the name.

Sir James Dyson went through over 5,126 prototypes over the course of 15 years before creating the self-named Dyson best-selling bagless vacuum cleaner that led to a net worth of **$4.5 billion.**

Steven Spielberg, in all his cinematic genius, has produced films that have grossed over 9 billion dollars. Surprisingly enough, he was rejected not once, but *twice* from the USC School of Cinematic Arts.

No Disney? That would be true if doubt controlled this young man. Walt Disney was told by his newspaper editor "that he lacked imagination and had no good ideas." Failure over doubt?

Dr. Seuss, whom we all know and love with stories that rhyme from beginning to end, was rejected 27 times when attempting to publish his first book. Would you have given up after the 15th rejection? What about the 20th rejection? His rejected books have now sold over 600 million copies world-wide.

Michael Jordan, as everyone knows, was cut from his high school basketball team. Getting cut can create a tremendous amount of doubt. In his own words, "On 26 occasions I have been entrusted to take the game winning shot, and I missed. I have failed over and over again in my life. And that is why I succeed." Michael Jordan is arguably the best basketball player to ever play.

As stated by Albert Einstein, failure is just success in progress. If you'd rather not fail, you will probably never be successful.

This is a very short list of many ultra-successful people who are no strangers to failure. I pray that one day your name will find itself among this list. One day, your story will inspire others to fail towards success as they learn about all you have overcome. This is what the future can have in store for you.

"Defeat (failure) is a state of mind; no one is ever defeated until defeat has been accepted as a reality." Failure in anything is merely temporary. Defeat (failure) simply tells me that something is wrong in my doing; it's a path leading to success"—Bruce Lee

Everyone on this list has failed and failed often. What have we learned?

DOUBT WILL KILL MORE DREAMS THAN FAILURE EVER

As you consider your potential greatness, ask yourself if you *really* believe that you are good enough to be successful. If so, with your faith anchored in Christ every failure is simply a part of the blueprint that Christ has for success.

The final story I'd like to share is mine. I am the owner and founder of the math tutoring center Double A+ Tutorials where our slogan is "We make math simple." Riding the success of our first store we opened a second center while looking for the location for a third. Then COVID-19 hit. It put the second location out of business. We were never able to recoup our investment in that location for the buildout, the advertisement, the signage, the architectural and attorney fees and more. All said we lost thousands and thousands of dollars at that location. It was a horrific failure. The first location was on life support and has made its way to the intensive care unit; however, it is still alive and open, and Christ can do a lot with just our little. Looking at the monumental success of those before me who endured epic failure, I am reminded and assured that we are right on schedule for a Double A+ Tutorials multi-million-dollar Hollywood success story. Please keep your eyes and ears open and someday soon you will see a Double A+ in your city.

Success is not relegated to mythical people that you can't talk to or communicate with.

To everyone reading this message I offer you my personal email as I would love to hear from you when you achieve the success you are pursuing. Likewise, I would love to hear from you if you are struggling and need some encouragement.

(jstephens@wemakemathsimple.com)

CALL TO ACTION:

I want you to define your goal. Identify your personal doubt (fear). Pray for guidance and pursue it with unyielding determination.

May God bless you in all your endeavors and whatever you pursue. Always remember to pursue Christ first and understand that He is the source to all that you are.

Jerry Stephens

P.S.

The young man took the shot and unlike the fairytale ending, he missed. *AGAIN*. Not only did he miss, he shot another airball. Yes, 4 airballs. As a result of that missed shot, his team lost and was eliminated from the playoffs. When asked how his off season went after missing those shots, the young man replied, "I didn't have an off season. I went straight to the high school gym that night as soon as we landed, and the janitor opened the gym for me. I was there until the sun came up. And went back there the next day and the next day and the next day after that…" Not only did he fail, but his failure was on national television, and he failed horribly. He shot 4 airballs in a critical and game winning situation. Remember, failure doesn't kill dreams-- doubt does.

The young man that shot the 4 airballs went on to become arguably 1 of the top 5 basketball players in NBA history. His name is Kobe Bryant.

NOTES

FEAR

By: Jalen Christopher

College Student

There is a first time for everything: first job, first love, first game, first day. It's common to get anxious about new experiences and fear how they may turn out. What happens over time is that you have more new experiences. The completion of each experience helps you to realize how capable and successful you can be. When we exercise courage, we act. With each action taken, confidence is built, and fear disappears.

Fear can feel like the devil on your shoulder telling you that you should not try something because it may turn out negative for you. Fear can stop you from talking to your crush, because of the possibility of rejection.

Sometimes the feeling of fear can be useful in life. The world is a scary place, and there are things in this world that truly cause us harm. There are people and experiences that fear protects us against. Fear can sometimes save us like a life jacket that keeps you afloat in the world.

Fear can cause problems in our lives. If you live your life playing it safe, you will eventually grow feelings of resentment for not having taken the risks. It is the first step down the sad road of bitterness. There is that old saying of "should've, could've, would've, but didn't." that will play out in your mind. The result of you playing it safe turns into someone else getting the promotion, the girl, or that which is desirable to you. It becomes a prison of your own making.

To conquer your fears, you must build courage and act. Being fearful may be a bad habit that you have allowed to occupy your life. How do you stop a habit that has been the foundation of your life? One step at a time. The best way to fix a problem is to recognize the problem. Scale how big the problem is. Scale how capable you are and negotiate with yourself to see what you could do. An easy way to think of this is to imagine you are having a conversation with yourself so that you fix the problem in a way that won't make you hate yourself. Let's say you want to get into shape, had you known you'd lose weight and feel better, if you only went on a run every so often. Well, you might talk to yourself and say, "Hey, I want to exercise more. I want to lose this weight. What if I ran a mile a day?" You would then say to yourself, "That's crazy because I haven't run a mile since P.E. in middle school!" You would then lower your terms, "How about half a mile?" "No!" you would reply. "How about we jog for two minutes, and then walk the rest of the mile?" You think, "I can jog for two minutes. Deal."

CALL TO ACTION:

When changing a habit, it is best to do it in small increments. To negotiate in a way that is manageable and easily replicable. So here is the challenge, find a problem. Negotiate with yourself in a way that betters yourself in a way you want to be better. Watch your improvement over the course of two weeks and watch yourself as your life improves.

NOTES

PRODUCING LIFE

By: Jared Black

Music Producer

Producing life is not so much about life happening to you. Rather, it's how you happen to life within the situations presented to you. At least that's what I've surmised in my 25 years of living. Everyone has a hobby; a certain activity they like, maybe even love doing. Some people like fishing, and some like bowling. Some people love dancing, and some love trolling. Personally, I love producing music, whether it be making beats, or editing songs for different artists. I love how I can take many different elements of music and combine them to form sounds good to listen to, as well as create something never heard. I love how these music creations can make people feel. Some music evokes feelings of sadness, while a different piece of music may evoke feelings of gladness. Other possible feelings that can be produced include excitement and anger. Music can bring forth feelings of sympathy as well as empathy. The reason I'm telling you this is not to advertise the cool aspects of being a music producer, but rather to show the similarities between music production and life.

In life, different situations are presented to us every day. These situations may cause us to feel different emotions just as music does. The same sadness, gladness, excitement, anger along with many more emotions. No matter what situation is presented to us, it is up to us to take that situation and make the best out of it. Doing this will produce a happier life for ourselves in the long run. It helps us to keep a positive mindset throughout any circumstance. The negative effects of stress and worry on the human body are well researched and documented. On that account, it is to our great benefit that we reduce the amount of stress and worry in our lives. No one can control the things that happen to them in life, not one hundred percent of the time at least. We can control how we react to these events. Therefore, life is not so much what you make it, rather what you can make out of all the situations presented to you.

CALL TO ACTION:

This upcoming week, I would like you to practice positive thinking after every eventful situation. No matter if the event is good or bad, practice positive thinking. Take the negative and turn it into a positive. Also, try and take the positive and learn from that event as well. Do this after every noteworthy event and you will be on your way to a happier, more stress-free life.

NOTES

QUESTIONS

By: K.W. James

Business Owner

O n your bookcase is a book which you have never read. In this book is the glories, wonders, tragedies, and triumphs of Barrack Obama. If that book sits unread on your bookshelf the content of it is external to you and your understanding of him. Let's say that one day you decide to take it down and begin to read it. To your surprise, you are thrilled by the book, fascinated, and moved emotionally by it. The events in the book captivate your attention and now they stick with you like a hog wallowing in mud. All the great lines and sayings remain clearly in your memory.

Whenever you want to, you retrieve that wonder from inside yourself, dwell on it, and use it as food for your mind and heart. Once this book was outside you and now it is inside you, and you can feed upon it anytime your mind desires it.

It is that way with any great experience in life. It remains external until we take it within ourselves. If you were fascinated by that book, I have another book, that when read and studied, will blow you away. But with this book, you must ask questions to get into the very core of its teaching.

Webster Dictionary gives this definition of the word "Question"; "A sentence in an interrogative form addressed to someone in order to get information in reply."

The book I am recommending can be utilized in a classroom setting. There can be multiple people in the classroom, or just one person. The question-and-answer scenario is the same regardless of how many people are in the setting.

For our example, the bible is our book of choice for this discussion. Before asking questions about any subject, it is a good rule of practice to research the subject yourself first. It is extremely important to do a self-examination of your intentions before reading this book. Why? Because this book will challenge you in ways of life and thinking unlike anything you will ever read and study again. Here are a few questions you must ask yourself before and while reading this book.

What is my motive for reading this book?

Will I ask questions for clarity when reading?

Words have meanings. Do I have a clear understanding of the words?

What do I plan to do with the information?

How will I use the information?

If the information does not meet my satisfaction, how will I respond?

Am I open minded or closed minded?

Have I already made up my mind before receiving the answer?

If I do not understand, will I keep asking additional questions until I do understand?

CALL TO ACTION:

Let's get started. I will help you along the way. Do not jump ahead, complete each step before going to the next step.

Step I. Read Ephesians 1:1-3

Step II. Write a brief paragraph about the first three verses. In the paragraph, express what the passages are saying and what do they mean to you.

Step III. Ask a family member about the first three verses: Ask then this Question: What do the first three verses say? What is the thought expressed? How do you use this today (How does this apply to your daily life)?

Ok. Now let's get to the core of these verses by asking some questions.

Verse one: What is the meaning of "apostle", "Jesus", Christ", "the will" and "saints"?

Verse two: What is the meaning of "Grace", "peace" and "Lord"?

Verse three: What is the meaning of "Blessed" when referring to "God" and when referring to "us" in this verse.

Step IV. Write the meaning of these words on another page.

Step V. Definitions of the following words in these verses.

"apostle" – sent out, to send out, sent

"Jesus" – savior, deliverer

"Christ" – Anointed (to anoint something or someone means, "approval")

"the will" – something that God has put in place to bring about the results He desires

"saints" – set apart, separated ones

"Grace" – granted unearned favor

"peace" – all is well between you and God

"Lord" – master

"Blessed"- honor, to speak well of

Step VI. Study the words in **Step V** and rewrite your paragraph from **Step II** with the meaning of these words and share it with someone. Before rewriting your new paragraph there are some questions you must think about first.

Questions

Verse 1: Who sent Paul out? Who gave Paul his message? Why is that important? Who is Paul writing to? What words does Paul use to describe his audience?

How does this (words used to describe his audience) help them to accept his words?

Verse 2: What two words does Paul use to help his audience know how what God thinks of them? How does these two words help you know what God thinks of you?

Verse 3: What is Paul saying when he states, "Blessed be the God" and "who has blessed us"? How has God blessed us in this verse? Where are all these blessings found?

Now, rewrite your paragraph with an understanding of the words in Step V and having consideration of the questions above. Share this new paragraph with the person you asked above.

NOTES

HOW TO BECOME A RELIABLE YOUNG MAN

By: Shelton Gibbs III

Minister

I hope it is your desire to become a great man someday. But you must begin now, it does not happen by accident, it can only happen if you start being a person anyone can rely on now.

Definition

The word reliable has its origins in relier, Old French for fasten or attach, the reliable man was an immovable pillar of strength on which you could hang your hat, someone you could lean and depend on, a man you could trust.

If a man is unreliable, he is like a clock missing some numbers.

If a man is unreliable, he is about as useful as an ashtray on a motorcycle.

Proverbs 11:3

Integrity guides decent people, but hypocrisy leads treacherous people to ruin.

I. How is Reliability Developed

To be a reliable man it starts with being a **responsible son:** obedient to parents, helpful around the house, keeping your room clean, mowing the yard, and taking out the trash.

To be a reliable man it starts with being **a good student**: getting to school with books, paper, pencils, pens and going to all assigned classes, and being on time. Paying attention to the teacher's instruction. Taking good notes and turning in homework on time; determining to make good grades.

To be a reliable man, begins with being an **excellent athlete,** following the coach's instruction; being a team player. Practice hard, even on your own. Give 110 percent to all you do. Never play dirty, always according to the rules.

To be a reliable man, includes being a **good citizen:** volunteer and be active in your community, be honest and trustworthy, follow rules and laws, respect the rights of others, be informed about the world around you, respect the property of others, be compassionate, and take responsibility for your actions.

To be a reliable man, it includes being a **Christian**, following the word of God. Give your life to Christ early. Own a bible and read it. Develop a prayer life depending on God for everything. Don't be ashamed to work in the church, Volunteer to usher, read scripture, lead songs. Participate in the youth group and be a leader to other youth.

II. Remember the following scriptures and live by them.

Ecclesiastes 12:1 "Remember now thy Creator in the days of thy youth, while the evil days come not, nor the years draw nigh, when thou shalt say, I have no pleasure in them;"

Proverbs 3:1-5 "My son, do not forget my teaching, but let your heart keep my commandments, for length of days and years of life and peace they will add to you. Let not steadfast love and faithfulness forsake you; bind them around your neck; write them on the tablet of your heart, so you will find favor and good success in the sight of God and man. Trust in the Lord with all your heart, and do not lean on your own understanding, in all your ways acknowledge Him and He will direct your steps."

Psalm 119:9 "How can a young man keep his way pure? By guarding it according to your word."

Ecclesiastes 11:9 "Rejoice, O young man, in your youth, and let your heart cheer you in the days of your youth. Walk in the ways of your heart and the sight of your eyes. But know that for all these things God will bring you into judgment."

1 Timothy 4:12 "Let no one despise you for your youth, but set the believers an example in speech, in conduct, in love, in faith, in purity."

Romans 12:2 "Do not be conformed to this world, but be transformed by the renewal of your mind, that by testing you may discern what is the will of God, what is good and acceptable and perfect."

III. 15 Maxims for being a Reliable Man

CALL TO ACTION: *(choose one and work on it daily)*

1. Keep your promises.

2. Don't overpromise.

3. Manage expectations.

4. Don't leave other people hanging.

5. Whatever you do, do it well.

6. Be consistent.

7. Finish what you start.

8. Pull your weight and shoulder your own responsibilities.

9. Be honest.

10. Pay back money and return things in a timely manner.

11. Be punctual.

12. Be fair and consistent in rewards and punishments.

13. Don't let circumstance dictate your behavior.

14. Don't collapse in emergencies.

15. Show up

If you follow the things shared, there is absolute greatness in store for you!

NOTES

SENSE OF HUMOR

By: Otis Idlebird

Entrepreneur

One human trait I believe is good to have, is a sense of humor. Humor is the quality of being amusing. It is expressed in literature and speech. Wikipedia defines humor as, "the tendency of experiences to provoke laughter and provide amusement." When one uses humor in their daily communication it can make a conversation interesting by seeking and successfully implicating funny moments in the things, people, and actions around them.

There are many ways to address this topic of humor. I would like to deal specifically with a funny personality. This kind of personality simply deals with a person being genuinely funny to his or her peers. Being able to define humor in the things around you does not have to be dark, insulting, demeaning or outright rude, just simply silly.

It is hard to try and instruct someone to be funny. To some, it just comes naturally. For most, I believe, it is developed overtime.

A lot of my humor came from childhood experiences. I am one of six children. I remember we would always have some type of adventure going on in our household, which brought about some very funny times. I grew up in a time where we would get up on Saturday mornings and watch cartoons. This gave us the opportunity to mimic some of the things that we would see on TV. I come from a time where we would get the comic strips in the newspaper. I would get a kick out of reading all the different comics that the newspaper offered. Garfield, Dennis the Menace, Spiderman, Charlie Brown, and many other comics were my favorite! These characters, in my opinion, possessed a very simple humor, short enough and funny enough to fill in those little white bubbles that were placed by everyone's image to express speech as they dealt with life's circumstances in a humorous way. Adding a bit of humor to those actions were funny and helped to shape how a young boy sees the world, not growing up too fast, but being able to be silly in the moment.

Those times also helped me to be able to laugh at myself as I visualized those images and saw myself in those actions. When reality is mixed with imagination, some of those things happening in real life triggers a memory of those comical renderings in the newspaper and brings about a laugh, as I play out those things in real life. Boy, what a laugh I would experience in the end!

Humor has been able to hide painful moments as well. Have you ever been distracted by humor before receiving a shot in the arm? The humor takes your mind off the pain you are about to experience. It can also lessen the impact of bad news. Are you sitting down? Do you want the good news or the bad news first? Sometimes conversations would start off this way before the tough conversations started. Scary situations are made bearable when you chant to yourself, "It's not real!" Humor is also able to comfort the hearts of those who are sad. I use humor when I am nervous. Many times, just before I get ready to speak publicly, I think of something funny to say to get rid of the butterflies I may have in my stomach. When humor comes naturally, there is no need to prepare for how conversations could go, but it doesn't hurt to look at different joke books as you prepare for a public speaking engagement. I believe that if the world would laugh a lot more together, it would make a lot of things just a little easier to talk about, and to deal with.

Humor is very effective when trying to get over being nervous about meeting someone that you have a crush on. You have the ability to weigh in your mind the many ways to blunder the whole experience. Just be your silly self. I find that you will laugh inside yourself and if you are brave enough to share your thoughts with the person you're interested in, it can be a great icebreaker. Being able to laugh in a relationship is priceless. I am sure that you all have more to laugh about in a relationship than to fuss about. I am aware that there are situations that can arise in a relationship that are not funny. Surely, I am not talking about those moments of trials that must be seriously worked out and overcome. I am referring to the daily interaction of two individuals that are merging two points of view of a circumstance. To be able to laugh at some of the things that you experience on a particular day can have amazing results. Our mind can entertain different scenarios and outcomes. Sometimes, your inner thoughts add a bit of levity within you but may or may not be funny to others. Just be thankful that offensive thoughts never got past your lips. There are times when you can get to be too silly, but at any rate, being able to laugh in a relationship is a good thing.

Watching TV shows and movies that are written for humor and laughter for the audience typically go over well because they aim to make light of circumstances that are real in nature. Romantic and situational comedy shows are made to make fun of things around us. For the most part, they go over well, but there is a dark side to humor that I encourage you NOT to take part in. Its design is to cause one to feel small, bullied, and ashamed in its delivery. Jokes can sometimes seem naughty, dirty, and profane.

In the book of [Ephesians 5:4 KJV] "Neither filthiness, nor foolish talking, nor jesting, which are not convenient: but rather giving of thanks."

The Apostle Paul, as he begins to establish the kind of Christian behavior that is acceptable, wants the individual to understand that you can be very humorous and silly in your disposition as you deal with other people. Sometimes circumstances that you may see in the world around you and in people you spend your time with can be unacceptable to God. Paul says that at no time should your talking become foolish or filthy, nor should you have jokes which are not convenient and off-putting. He says, "I would rather you spend that energy giving thanks to the Lord for all that he has done. When we have in mind to be pleasing to the Lord with this mouth that he blessed us with, it eliminates some of the foolishness that we sometimes stoop down to, even when we joke with one another. So, it is OK to be funny! It is OK to be silly!

Christians, in my opinion, are some of the funniest people in the world! When our conversations dip into the darker areas of humor and foolish talking, I believe we venture into conversations that do not represent God. This type of humor does not represent His purpose for mankind and is a misrepresentation of his ability and power in this world in which we live. I believe it is also degrading and demeaning to his creation, which is mankind. The Lord said that we should not be involved with foolish talk and joking. So, using foolish talking and saying I was just joking is unacceptable.

CALL TO ACTION:

You should not tell stories that are not true to bring about laughter. You don't have to utilize false stories to be funny. The stories do not have to disrespect an individual, their family, or their parents to be funny either. This kind of behavior has caused many people to be sad or even take their own lives. So, as you go about your daily life, be funny, be silly and don't grow up too fast. Enjoy seeing the world through the eyes of a child, young boy, teenager, and later, a young man, bringing laughter into the world genuinely. Make sure you stay away from conversations and joking that are disgraceful to the Lord. I believe that you will be the life of the party and not one who seeks to hurt others through the things that you do and speak.

NOTES

RHINO MENTALITY

By: Jason E. Christopher

Healthcare/Entrepreneur/CEO of Me

"Our Mentality Becomes Our Reality!" – Billy Cox

I am fascinated by many animals, but the Rhinoceros is my favorite! Honestly, it is the unattractive qualities of the Rhino that I love and relate to the most. Let's talk about these qualities that the normal person would consider disadvantages, but how we see them as necessary attributes for success. Rhinos: their vision is not the best, they like to roll around in mud, they typically travel alone. These don't sound like desirable qualities… take a closer look. Let's see how these qualities fit into the Rhino Mentality!

To see far away I need to wear glasses, I rarely wear them unless I am driving. So typically, when I am at work, I will identify people by the way they walk, stand, or move. Over the years I have gotten pretty good at adapting to not seeing clearly. Rhinos are not made to see very far! Most experts say that their vision is not the best. How does having poor eyesight help with a Rhino Mentality? I am glad you asked…those same experts go on to say that what they lack in vision has heightened their sense of smell and hearing. This alerts them when other animals or humans come around. Rhinos charge when they smell something that does not belong. Rhinos will charge at a tree and even a rock, it does not matter if you are something that he thinks doesn't belong… he's coming at you! Limited sight limits distractions! Rhino Mentality!

Have you ever had someone look at you confused because they had no idea what you were doing… but you knew what you were doing so it did not matter? Join the club, Rhinos love to roll around in mud. Why does an over 2-ton majestic beast enjoy covering himself in mud? What the common person would think is disgusting, the Rhino thinks protection. The mud acts as a protective barrier to the Rhinos already thick skin. Without the protective layer of mud, the skin of the Rhino is vulnerable to the burn of the sun and the bite of insects. The mud keeps the sun from burning his skin and the bugs from constantly biting. Rhino Mentality!

Consider the failures, disappointments, and let downs in your life as mud. Embrace them…wear them as badges of honor… don't let the mud defeat you or get you down… but let it act as a barrier to protect you from all the naysayers, doubters, and haters. Let the mud help to protect you from the insects in your life that want to drain you. Rhinos don't see failures; they see opportunity for more protection from outside forces that want to do him harm. Rhino Mentality!

Rhinos go it alone. The male Rhino is a solitary animal that will dominate an area but will occasionally form a group called a "crash". This crash normally consists of a female and her offspring. The male Rhino will allow some sub-dominate males to live on his territory. Rhino Mentality! Being a Rhino can be lonely but even Rhinos allow others to be in their space at times. Those that are allowed in their space must be headed in the same direction and be like-minded. The term crash, for a group of Rhinos, originated from when Rhinos moved together, they would take everything in their path out. Go it alone unless those around you are headed in the same direction. Rhino Mentality!

Always have a Rhino Mentality! What doesn't kill you, makes you stronger! Yes, you may run into trees and rocks on the way but always - Swing for the fences! Babe Ruth is known for his ability to hit home runs… but his batting average was horrible! So many strikeouts yet known for homeruns. Rhinos go ALL in! So, Rhino Up & Go Charge!!!

CALL TO ACTION:

Know who YOU are and what YOU want! This week unplug – NO social media! No television! Positive messages ONLY!

Unplug 1 day = Baby Rhino

Unplug 7 days = Rhino in the making

Unplug 30 days = Rhino Mentality!!!

Listen to the following for the next 7 days:

Day 1: Start here - https://youtu.be/vfroyTkX-Fw

Day 2: https://youtu.be/E4mXeQ4DSfo

Day 3: https://youtu.be/-dVbkxekzKA

Day 4: https://youtu.be/kBLQRw9Z0Mc

Day 5: https://youtu.be/FncTDZxNbM4

Day 6: https://youtu.be/CMPGw7jhHPA

Day 7: https://youtu.be/PnYPOg538qA

Inspirational Song Bonus: https://youtu.be/tu9j_n0gihE

ET Bonus: "You Owe You!" - https://youtu.be/7Oxz060iedY

NOTES

SETTING OBJECTIVES

By: Ernie D. Seay

Owner of Run Your Dreams

Who told you that it couldn't be done?

Who said, If I were you, I wouldn't even try it?

The haters and naysayers are going to be around for a long time. Especially if you're looking to better yourself and your surroundings.

Setting goals is essential to moving from point A to point B and beyond.

Your goals can be huge, small, long term, or short term. You can have objectives that you need to hit today or this week that will move you towards whatever it is you're trying to achieve. Look at the end goal, then break it down into manageable tasks.

Some of you already know how to set goals and plan it out to make sure you hit your timeline. For others, this may be your first exposure to goal/objective setting. Here is a real-life example.

I run marathons. If a marathon (26.2 miles) is in 24 weeks, I set the date in my mind and write it down on something I see daily. I then set checkpoints. Running, stretching, eating, lifting and rest are all a part of my 24-week training plan. I didn't just jump off the sofa one day and run a marathon. I had to develop the right behaviors to get to 26.2 miles. Having Asthma hindered my progress at first, but getting into a rhythm of behaviors, allowed me to develop those skills necessary to complete over 20 marathons.

Daily, weekly, and monthly plans are then put in place, and I get started. There is something to be done daily that will push me towards the objective, the marathon. Some days are better than others, you may be highly productive a few days straight and then get thrown off course. It happens, the key is not to get so distracted and disappointed that you stop all together. When you get off course, check yourself, find out how you got off course and then self-correct.

There are perceived boundaries that others put on us and there are some that we put on ourselves. Pushing past those perceived boundaries is going to take work. It's going to require you to dig deep inside your core to bring out what you know is in you. It will be frustrating, you might even say, it's not worth it. It is worth it. Giving up on your goals is not an option. Get in the habit of setting goals, put a time limit on reaching them and then get to work.

Whatever you do, don't listen when someone says, your goals are too big. They may be too big for them, but for you, it's go time.

They are your goals, your dreams and it's up to you to embrace them and get started on reaching them.

CALL TO ACTION:

Set a goal for this week, it could be to read a book, do all your chores without having to be told to do, start an online savings account, fill out a college application, learn 5 new words. Whatever the goal, write it down, look at it every day, and do something towards that goal daily to move you to hitting that goal by the end of the week.

NOTES

2ND QUARTER

LEARNING & BALANCE

"AQ VS IQ"

By: Johnny L. Hawkins, Esq.

"The Warrior Lawyer"

Most of us are familiar with the acronym IQ" which stands for Intelligence Quotient, and measures just how smart you are. But most of us have never even heard of the acronym "**AQ**", which stands for **Adversity or Adaptability Quotient**, which measures one's ability to properly manage and deal with the adversities that he/she will encounter during their lifetime. Psychologists have indicated that overall success depends on 20% IQ; and 80% EQ and AQ (i.e., one's Emotional and Adversity Quotients). So let me say this to you RIGHT NOW regardless of how young you may be: it's awesome to be smart and to get real good grades while in school; but it's the individuals with the highest "AQ, that family, friends, your future bosses or clients, the ladies (lol), and the world-at-large will lean on the most from you They will come to you for comfort when the going gets rough; and trust me, it will. That is just a part of life.

What part of life you may be asking yourselves? The tests, trials, and tribulations of life. For it is in the tests and during the trials and tribulations of life that we go through that help make us and show us who we really are. The tests of life ultimately create the person, and moreover, show the true character of a man. This is an undeniable truth.

We must go through and overcome these tribulations of life. Young man, this is a universal law. And more importantly, God tells us directly, throughout His holy word.

I have been classified as smart most of my life, both while maneuvering in the streets, as well as while in the classroom and the boardroom. I mean seriously, I've been either designated, nominated, or appointed the leader of street clubs or gangs, the captain of certain sports teams, the designated president of certain formal school organizations such as student government the debate team, the appointed manager while on the job or special assignment, a squad leader during my boot camp and/or basic training experience after I joined the military. And now, in my professional career, I find myself blessed to be a nationally recognized "TOP 100 Trial Attorney in the USA."

Let me tell you all a BIG secret, the real deal. I did not just mention nor list the above accomplishments to be boastful or braggadocious; and more importantly, "NO" I do not attribute my many accomplishments to me being so-called "smart or intelligent". Nope, not at all! I personally attribute most, if not all, of my life accomplishments to date, to me being blessed by God to have been given a very high AQ. To state it more plainly, anytime I am tested, I refuse to give up, and I really can't stand losing, although the latter happens to even the best on occasion.

To be less than great in anything that I put my mind to is unacceptable. I personally find being average to be boring: average is just not for me, and it should not be something that appeals to you either. I find excellence to be stimulating and super-exciting! It is the "pursuit of excellence" that should help you get out of bed every morning, and that gets you the "good attention" the fanfare, the ladies, the crown, the popularity, the real big dough Most importantly, it has been my personal experience that it is *the pursuit of excellence* that will give you a true feeling of pride and makes you feel extremely good about yourself.

But guess what? Excellence only comes to those that when tested, pass both the smallest and the largest tests in life with mostly "A's"; because when it's all said and done and the dust settles, the person with the high AQ then appreciates the tests and the experiences, and comes out of the tests with a better attitude and a thankful heart towards God. This individual appreciates the very fact that not only did they make it or pass yet another life test, but that they excelled. In short, when it is over, they know within themselves that they kicked butt! And having this ability is all about having the right "ATTITUDE". Oh, don't get it twisted, Attitude is everything! Yes, you will be tested; and yes, there will be times when you feel that the tests are unfair; and yes, you may find yourself wanting to ask yourself the big question: "why me"? That is normal young man. But remember this: it is your test, and it will be your overall attitude, and your ability to adjust and adapt quickly (your "AQ") that will determine your outcome. In closing, my advice to each of you is simple: put real work and lots of effort into building up a high AQ. Trust me, you will never regret it

CALL TO ACTION:

Work on getting your minds and attitudes right and ready for life's tests to come, both small and large. Life will surely bring them your way. For remember, we are all, as humans, tested on a regular. When I use the word "test" I'm referring to any challenge or task that is put before you. So how do you get ready? By working on your attitude and your overall ability to adapt and adjust when things, good or bad, come your way.

This week, when you face a test, any so-called test, immediately identify it as just that: A TEST! Then work to adjust your overall attitude and mindset, and simply say to yourself, "I will pass this test with "Straight A's." If you get into the habit of doing this, then life's tests or challenges, both big or small, at least for you, will seem way more manageable and you will excel. Those around you will wonder how you always manage to do what you do; but you will know that it is because you've made it a priority to work on, improve upon and build up your "AQ" my young brother.

NOTES

THE GENERALIST USING YOUR GOD GIVEN TALENTS TO EXCEL

By: Patrick H. Worthey, Jr.

Minister

Years ago, in my hometown of Lubbock, Texas, I found myself walking home one warm summer evening on what was then Quirt Avenue. I do not know what prompted it, however, I began praying to God as I walked and as I prayed, my voice began to tremble as my words were altered by tears and crying. I was 14 years old at the time. My prayer to God was for him to use me mightily in his kingdom, the church, and that I would give my best to him in service to the kingdom.

From my time as a young child, even to this day, I have always had an unexplainable love for the Lord and his Church. Even now there are times in which I pray to God in tears wanting to give of the best of my talents and abilities to Him. On many occasions over the years, I have looked back to that evening with great thankfulness of how God has answered my prayer in so many ways. I suppose you could say this is my passion. Passion is something I believe every young man should have. By Passion,

I mean a great love or devotion to something for which you are willing to devote time and effort. You may even embody as a personal characteristic.

As I look back on my life, I have had several loves or interests which I would classify as passions, and by at least some definition could be considered a talent or ability. Early on, sports were a passion of mine. I have played football, basketball, run track, and at one time was an avid tennis player. In my adult life I became quite passionate about golf. At an early age I developed a love for public speaking which later, combined with a love for the word of God, has parlayed into a love for preaching. Other passions or even talents which developed in me were singing, working with young people and general ministry to people.

Passions are so valuable for each of us. It is within our passions that we develop a solid purpose. I define passion as my reason(s) for living. Purpose must fuel our lives. The wise man, Solomon gave perhaps the most profound definition of purpose in Ecclesiastes 12:13, he states: ". Now let us hear the conclusion of the whole matter, fear God and keep his commandments, for this is the whole duty (purpose) of man". The purpose of which Solomon speaks should be my ultimate purpose. It addresses this life and the life to come. It is my belief that all my passions should support my purpose, and simply put, my purpose is centered in my life in Christ. The Apostle Paul states this in Philippians 1:21 as he declares; "For me to live is Christ and to die is gain." I once came across a very profound statement that relates to this thought by Paul which states "Death is only a tragedy when one has not lived." I believe that true living in this life can only occur when one returns their talents and abilities to the one who supplied them to us in the first place. Whatever your talent or ability may be, consider it an obligation and distinct privilege to offer it enthusiastically to God.

I never thought that an early love of singing and leading songs to inner city children on a bus ministry would lead later to work in Youth Ministry. A love for public speaking combined with a love for God and his word at an early age would lead to a lifetime of preaching. A love of people would lead to a passion for ministry. Even as funny as it seems, a past passion of athletics, specifically track, would lead to the portrayal of a fictional "Superhero" known as "Bible Man" as I run down the aisles of the church auditorium during the yearly Vacation Bible School to the apparent enjoyment of the youth, as well as some adults.

CALL TO ACTION:

These and other experiences not mentioned all point back to that warm summer evening and my prayer that God would use me mightily in his kingdom. I would encourage any young man to utter this same prayer and offer up to God all your talents and abilities. I fully believe that in doing so, you will be amazed at what God will do in return.

Give him all your best!

NOTES

UNDERSTANDING PEOPLE

By: Jared Christopher

College Student

They say if you want to make God laugh, tell him your plans. You are destined for greatness. All the plans God has for you will not come about without trials and tribulations. Throughout your journey of life, you will go through dark times and will encounter people that will either lift you up or try to tear you down. Luckily, God has specifically placed every person you have ever crossed paths with to mold you into the person he plans for you to be when called into greatness. Therefore, one of the most important skills in life is being able to understand people.

The first step of mastering the skill of understanding people begins with understanding yourself. Everything starts with your mindset. You need to get yourself right before you can go out into the world and analyze other people. You need to discover what characteristics God blessed you with. This is important because once you are aware of your qualities, you can then work on the less developed areas of yourself. For example, as an introverted, calm, and careful person, you would work on being extroverted, adventurous, and carefree. You want to use these qualities as tools whenever you meet people. You don't have to become this person, but it's good for you to have a toolbox in which all your qualities lie. Once you master the innate qualities that you were born with along with the opposite qualities you develop, your potential for impacting people's lives will be limitless.

Another important part of mastering this skill is knowing your buttons. Having a list of your known triggers is mandatory so you do not easily get out of character. I put special thought into identifying the things I stress over that may be important and the least important things. And so should you. All other challenges, you should try to adapt and accept. All you have is your peace, and you must do anything to protect it. Once you correctly separate the things that are important from things that are not, you are halfway there. The problems that used to rob you of your smile are suddenly irrelevant when you do this. Everyone has a list of things that drive them crazy, but since you made your list of things to be mindful of, childish actions of others will not affect you, whenever days come when people try to knock you off your pivot or purpose, you can remember your list of things that matter and the things that don't. Think of people looking for trouble, as levels in a game which you already have the cheat codes to. Now you can manage situations in life with ease. A large part of being a grown-up in the real world is having to engage with difficult people, while maintaining a positive attitude. Many people in jail right now are there because they did not control their emotions. Now they are stuck in a cage for however long. If you never learn to get control of yourself, there are two places that are always open and more than happy to take you; the gates to jail and the gates to hell.

Thirdly, another concept I want you to understand is that people are here for reasons and seasons. People will come and go like leaves on a tree. You must be able to embrace the lessons and qualities given to you because of the purpose they served in your life. If you have a friend that has a crazy work ethic but is also untrustworthy, it would be in your best interest to cut them off. You should still be thankful for the resourceful blessing they may have been for you. Even when a person feels like they do not want to be in your life, it is ok to let them go. People may leave our lives because we must make the conscious choice to remove them, or they may leave by their choice. Either way may be painful at times. God gives the hardest battles to his strongest soldiers. This means you may go through training courses in life so that you are ready for the battle's life has for you down the line.

In conclusion, these are great skills for life that I wish I had known when I was growing up. Keep in mind that the path to greatness is long and cold. Keep your chin up even if you walk down that road alone. Through the storms you can smile because you know God won't give you anything that you can't handle.

CALL TO ACTION:

I encourage you to first understand yourself, find out what makes you tick, then understand that people are here for reasons and for seasons. It is not an easy task but doing this will bring you one step closer towards your purpose.

NOTES

CODE SWITCHING

By: Brian Mattisons

Business Performance Advisor, Human Resources Outsourcing

It's truly an interesting time in the world today and navigating our world successfully requires men of color to view it through several lenses and languages. Men of color must navigate two worlds: black culture and majority (white) culture.

As human beings we develop an innate sense of survival. I'd argue that black men have developed this sense to the 10th power. A critical part to our survival is navigating social interactions; personal, professional, and educational. Black men (Black people) adjust their behavior based on with whom we are interacting.

Our behavior, speech, dress, or style may adjust based on our environment. Our conversation or interaction with people can be different whether being in a barbershop or a conference room. We are multi-lingual and often do not realize it. It is something that comes naturally. For example, how many times have you heard one Black person say to another; "You're trying to talk white? You may have also noticed having a casual conversation with your father or mother and they need to take a "work" call. What happens? Manner of speech changes or style of speech changes.

This type of adjustment of behavior is referred to as the "code-switch." "Code-switching," has long been a strategy for Black people to successfully navigate interracial interactions. It has a significant impact on our overall well-being and employment/business opportunities. It is suggested that code-switching often occurs to combat the negative stereotypes of Black people in terms of appropriate behavior or normal behavior for a specific environment.

For example, research conducted in schools suggests that Black students selectively code-switch between standard English in the classroom and African-American Vernacular English (AAVE) with their peers. This elevates their social standing with each intended audience. Black fathers encourage their Black sons to code-switch to survive interactions with the police. For example, do not question them, answer their questions clearly and concisely, don't use "street" talk or slang, and don't talk with your hands, etc.

Code-switching presents a dilemma for our young men. On one hand our young men want to remain "100" or "true", yet they are seeking to be accepted as equal in the larger society.

The Pew Research Center found that Black college graduates, especially under 50, found code-switching to be necessary.

Education and age were prominent in this opinion, with younger and more educated Black adults saying that code-switching was an important skill to have ~ Dunn, 2019.

The more education you have as a Black man, the less likely it is that you will see other Black men in your chosen field of work or study. The hard truth is, the more educated and successful you are, the less Black people you will see at the same level. There is an inverse relationship between higher education and Black men. Therefore, code-switching is a valued skill for Black men to have and leverage as they navigate the social and economic opportunities.

CALL TO ACTION:

In the weeks ahead, do not accept the statement of "trying to talk white." Embrace the fact you are multi-lingual and what it means within the strategy for your life. No other culture understands this or should understand this concept more than Black men. Embrace and expand this wonderful gift and use it to your advantage.

Dunn, Amina (2019, Sep 24). Younger, college-educated black Americans are most likely to feel need to 'code-switch'. Retrieved from:

https://www.pewresearch.org/fact-tank/2019/09/24/younger-college-educated-black-americans-are-most-likely-to-feel-need-to-code-switch/.

NOTES

ATTIRE; THE FIRST LESSON OF OWNERSHIP

By: Sydney Fears

Aerospace Engineer

Outdoor Gallant, LLC, Owner

I once awaited a big job interview, and I had every intention for my attire to be part of my impression. However, nothing was overly exceptional about my attire. Frankly, there were several other occasions when I had worn the same suit and tie. There was not anything ostensible about its brand or make. As I sat for the last round of interviews with the Vice President of the company, although I had rehearsed and was eager to present my skills, I was still a bit nervous. However, I remembered clearly that my attire gave me that last bit of confidence as a reminder of what I need not be nervous about. After my interview with the VP, he told me specifically that he intended to offer me the position. This was mostly due to what he candidly admitted. It was the way I dressed. and how I presented myself. This was my motivation from the very beginning, not simply the attire itself, but how I owned it. This experience reinforced a sensible conclusion that one of the first lessons of ownership is the ownership of your attire and the importance in the way you present yourself. It is like building a business except, it is the business of "self."

There are variables to the importance of how you present yourself that you must consider. "Attire" does not always mean "a suit and tie." The presentation of yourself can carry connotation outside of dress clothes, yet reinforce immensely when you apply this attire with your intention. The ownership of your attire and your presentation will reflect the value you place on yourself and your intentions. The more value you add will increase your proprietorship based on three major areas: posture and physique (which is the base of attire), your wardrobe (which is the basis of your attire), and your character and attitude (which fundamentally is the best attire you can have). These three areas all contribute to the importance in the way you present yourself.

Initially, the importance of how you present yourself starts with posture and physique. Correct posture, such as sitting, standing up straight, and communicating with direct eye contact, is a body language that has a significant impact on the impression of your attitude, confidence, energy level, and concern with self-image. Bad posture oftentimes communicates the direct opposite. Your posture is the first message you send to anyone, and it is important to convey the appropriate message not only in a professional environment but amongst your peers. Great posture is the fundamental way to take control and own your self-image irrespective of attire or special clothes. This gives you the edge in social and business interactions. Coupled with posture is physique. Given that we are all different shapes and sizes, this is relative to your personal ability and meant to be a goal for continual development from wherever you start.

The continuous improvement and development of your physique through exercise and healthy habits sets tone, impression, and builds reputation amongst others (also, irrespective of attire or special clothes). Simply, you look the best in your attire when you strive to look the best without it. Both posture and physique are the starting points in how you present yourself. With good posture and physique, any attire worn correctly will enhance the look. You may discover that an average dressed man with great posture and physique will stand out more than the finest dressed man with the opposite.

Secondly, the importance of how you present yourself continues with your actual dress wardrobe, which is the basis of your attire. Obviously, there are categories of attire suitable for various occasions; however, the focus here will be professional and business attire. It is never too early to start building a dress wardrobe and continually adding sophistication to your #52 collection. In both the competitive business world and special occasions, the right dress attire will always set you apart. The basic and most critical components of a dress wardrobe are a solid suit, a blazer, one pair of dress pants, a dress shirt, and a tie. You should strive to have one solid suit in your wardrobe that is navy blue, dark charcoal, or black, with a jacket that is single breasted with two or three buttons. Additionally, you should try to have at least one blazer in your wardrobe. A blazer is a solid-colored jacket that can be versatile and worn based on the formality of an occasion. One pair of dress pants should be black or dark charcoal. One dress shirt should be white with preferably a spread collar, which presents an efficient and neat look. Another great option is a solid light-blue dress shirt with a spread collar. Lastly, a solid-colored tie for the finishing touch. It is recommended that a tie for business be kept subtle while ties for social events can have more personal and creative flare.

As you mature in your dress wardrobe over time, sophistication will show within the intricate details. More sophisticated details to consider include watches, pocket squares, cufflinks, lapel pins, single or double-breasted suits, collar styles, dress shirt patterns, neck or bow ties, colors of ties and knot styles, suspenders, belt styles, sock patterns, and types of shoes. These details may or may not be overwhelming to you based on the level of sophistication you have added to your wardrobe already. However, these elements are meant to accentuate the basics of your attire.

The wardrobe components with a growing sophistication will help you develop the substance of how you define yourself through your attire, making the ownership of your attire an admirable display of how you present yourself. The importance of how you present yourself ends, most significant of all, with your character and attitude, which in a figurative way is the best attire you can own. Through a growing level of character and positive attitude, you truly own your attire. It is the secret ingredient that spells inner confidence, certainty, sincerity, and professionalism. In addition, it conveys humility, control, and charisma that accentuates your look to "speak" volumes without any spoken word. As you pursue greater levels of self-image through your evolving knowledge of attire and the way it reflects your character and attitude, continue to take ownership of the motivating factor to be greater and better than you were before. This allows you to consistently put your best "suit" forward any and everywhere you go. Together, with your basic wardrobe, good posture, and mindful physique, the world is yours.

CALL TO ACTION:

Step 1) Learn how to tie a tie (a different style knot if you already know how) or a bow tie. Investigate different collar-style dress shirts. Identify a type of a suit you like: two to three button suit or double-breasted suit. Think about a new dress ensemble and what you would be doing while dressed this way. Envision something great and make plans to get there by also thinking of the character and attitude that you may need to do so.

Step 2) On a morning that does not require you to dress up, go to a mirror and look at yourself. Then, put on dress clothes, preferably something from your basic wardrobe. Mentally record the difference of how you feel between the two. On a random day of the week, make plans to dress up and see what responses you receive from others. Allow this to build confidence and reinforce the positive elements of how attire and self-image can remain important to you.

NOTES

SPORTS AND LIFE BALANCE

By: Al Evans

Software Sales/Management

While thinking back on how we have raised our three oldest children as student athletes, we taught them to put God first, because through him all things are possible.

As it pertains to sports, it has been a true blessing. Once you have identified a sport that you truly love, make sure that you are committed to being the very best you can be through training, practice, effort and more importantly, hard work.

Achieving success in sports builds character and competitiveness which will help you tremendously in life. We have witnessed this firsthand through our three children.

There are sacrifices that you will have to make such as juggling school, practice, and your social life, it pays off in the long run. You may potentially get scholarships for college, excellent job opportunities, and may even play sports professionally. The Sky is the limit!

Listen to your parents because they know what is best. They can guide you in the right direction, whether they know the answers themselves or get those answers from others in your supportive circle. Your parents are going to be a big part of your success in sports and life in general.

CALL TO ACTION:

Based on whatever you learned in practice or training; you need to continue to apply those training exercises at home. The more repetition you have in anything you do in life, the better you are going to be. Have ongoing communication with your parents or someone that can help in assisting you with your training.

NOTES

GAMING

By: Tysen Wilson

Student

Video games are fun and all, but you need to find a balance between game and life. I'm not saying that you shouldn't play video games anymore, but you need to know life isn't just about playing games. I know there are days when you just do not want to do anything and just sit around. Like video games, you can't get better at things if you don't practice. Sometimes you play video games for hours, but there are other things you can be doing. One thing you can be doing is trying to find something else that you enjoy like sports, building things, or drawing.

Continue to dream and use your mind to think of new things you can do and try. You may enjoy it. Another thing you can do is try to better yourself with the time that you usually spend on video games. Do things around the house like working out or reading. You could always read about things that interest you or about things that are going on around you, so that you have more knowledge and education about whatever you're trying to do. Make sure to not just go through the motions. You need to get an understanding of whatever you are doing, so that you can use that knowledge whenever you need it.

CALL TO ACTION:

Make sure that you try to do something that helps you grow mentally and/or physically. The next time you are about to pick up your controller, think about switching it up and doing something to better yourself.

NOTES

FREE FROM PORNOGRAPHY

By: JB

When you hear the word slave, many of us revert to the 1800s when slavery was an acceptable or legal form of labor. As a slave you were property, you had no control, and were subject to the slave master's will. While the ownership of another human is now illegal in our society, the ideology of slavery is still deeply rooted in our minds. Whether we like it or not, we are all slaves to something. It could be work, your girlfriend, your possessions, money, yourself, etc.

In Luke 16:13, the Bible says, "No one can serve two masters. Either you will hate the one and love the other, or you will be devoted to the one and despise the other. You cannot serve both God and money." As you breakdown this verse, you see that the Bible says plainly that no matter what you think, or how you feel, it is inevitable that you will serve. Our whole purpose is to serve. Some of the world's greatest leaders apply themselves to what we call servant leadership. This helps us to understand that we will be a slave to someone or something. Now that we know that we all are slaves, or servants to something, we also must understand that we can't serve two different masters. Why can't I, you might ask? Well, if we look at the origin of the relationship between the slave and the slave master, the slave master gave the slave strenuous tasks that would require all or majority of their strength. Because the slave master owned you, it required you give him your all. Although we do not physically live by those rules today, what person you know works two 9-5's at the same time? It is impossible. Unlike the 1800s slavery, we get to choose whom we will serve, and because we can't serve two it is important to choose the right master. If you are reading this, it's very possible you and I have or had chosen the same master.

Pornography. "How can I be enslaved to pornography?" you might ask. Well, it's simple. If you urge to watch naked men and women have sex via the internet at every moment you get, then you're a slave. I've been there. Your bedtime is supposed to be 12 AM but because you started watching porn, at 11 o'clock your bedtime just extended from 12 to 3 o'clock. Many people believe porn is ok, it's natural. Let me tell you, there is nothing natural about watching people have sexual intercourse. Sexual intimacy, designed by God, is for the sharing between husbands and wives. Now, personally, I do not believe there's anything wrong with the curiosity of understanding the female or male body. Biology and nursing programs teach us this. But we all should know how to draw the line between curiosity and pleasure. As men we are visually stimulated so we must be vigilant about what we look at and indulge in.

Hundreds of people have become slaves to pornography. If you are struggling with this as well, you may be telling yourself, I understand that I'm a slave to pornography, but how do I free myself from this pornographic oppression? Actually, it is quite simple, but the process is difficult. Trust God. You may be thinking "Trust God, there's more to it than that?" Well, technically there is, but the answer to your freedom is God. The reason you got into a habitual pornographic diet in the first place is because you did not trust God with whatever situation or predicament you were in. I encourage you if you have the drive, it will take that drive to get away from this slave master and to trust God! Remember, "if it were easy, everybody would do it!"

Take time to really develop or reevaluate your relationship with God by reading your Bible. A great book in the Bible, I suggest you start with is Proverbs. Another habit to rely heavily on is prayer. I feel like a lot of times we underestimate the power of prayer. I, being a living testament of underestimating God and prayer, can say genuinely that prayer changes situations, mindsets, and point of views. For example, when you find yourself in the situation of being home alone and you feel tempted to use your private browser, a prayer might cause one of your parents to come home, or technical difficulties to occur with your private browser. Another example might be, when you find yourself sexually excited, a prayer might cause you to neglect your desire to masturbate or change your position of thought. You may think of how God or your parents think of the activity you are to indulge in. In addition, you also must understand that even though those examples might be your preferred outcome, there will be times when you fail.

In those moments of failure, it is important to have a community of accountable people you trust that will encourage you to get back up and fight! In the words of Will Smith, "fail forward!" Meaning, if you do fail learn why you failed and find multiple solutions to make sure you do not fail that way again!

CALL TO ACTION:

Celebrating small victories goes a long way! So even if it takes you three weeks to refrain for three consecutive days; celebrate because it is still a step forward. It takes drive, determination, perseverance, and most importantly God to break the chains of pornography. However, I guarantee you that when you do finally break free, God will bless you in ways than you cannot even imagine!

NOTES

BATTLING RACISM

By: J.R. Moore III

High School English Teacher

The thing about racism that makes it especially challenging to battle against is the fact that much of the battle must be fought internally. Yes, you read that correctly. This is a battle that must be fought from the inside out. Our deepest thoughts and innermost feelings carry a great amount of weight in this battle. This is not meant to deny the fact that we live in a society in which overt racism seems to run rampant externally. This is also not meant to imply that we are somehow responsible for the racist comments and actions that others perpetrate against us. It is instead meant to help us recognize that we are not powerless in these situations. We have more of a say in the way we are treated than we typically give ourselves credit for having. To truly understand this, we must look back into history a bit.

Long ago, when our predecessors were oppressed and abused, there was only one place they could go to escape the feelings of demoralization and despair. They had to look inward. There they found the strength to take a brutal whipping that was meant to break their spirit yet remained unbroken. It was there that they reminded themselves of their own humanity and worth. It was there that the plans were drawn up by many to escape and snatch back what had been stolen from them, their dignity and freedom. They could not wait for someone else to tell them that they deserved better. If that were the case, nothing would have ever changed.

In our case we must remember the same thing. Before we go to war to change our society, we must first answer some questions about ourselves. Do we believe that we are worth more than what we are receiving? Deep down on a fundamental level, do we truly believe it? This may sound like a silly question, but we must acknowledge that part of a racist society is the ingrained belief that one race is superior to all others. This belief is not only held by those who believe that they are superior, but it is passed down through generations to the "inferior" races as well. Over the course of hundreds of years, we have been taught to believe that we are inferior. Newspaper articles, scientific journals, and books have been written that purport to prove that we are a lesser race. Because of this long history of seeing and hearing these ludicrous falsehoods, we must acknowledge that we may have been tainted by thoughts of inferiority. And until we address those thoughts, we will not be able to win the battle. So how do we start?

First, we must be honest with ourselves about who we believe we are and what we believe we are worth. Then we must create an internal dialogue that expresses what someone of our great worth says or does in the face of racism. When we think of ourselves highly enough, we realize that certain things aren't even worth our time or energy. Comments do not affect us as much. Instead of taking them so personally, we see them as an unfortunate character flaw of whoever was foolish enough to utter such nonsense. It is then that we recognize the wisdom behind the saying, "It doesn't matter what they call you, it only matters what you answer to". And this is where the real battle is won.

Once we begin to truly believe that we are worthy, we walk a little differently, and talk a little differently. When the racists see this, they are disarmed. The only thing that they had to hold onto was this shameful belief that they were superior. And they will be forced to reckon with the fact that the only reason they had any power over us at all was that in some small parts of our minds, we believed it too. But no more. This causes them to suffer an identity crisis, internally. We stand up to them, undaunted, face to face, as equals in a way that we have never done before. Because this time we truly KNOW that we are equals. Once this is accomplished, we can go to work in earnest to accomplish our external goals. Once we have mastered ourselves internally, there is no external battle that we cannot win.

CALL TO ACTION:

- Write down your best qualities on one sheet of paper. Study your best qualities daily. Add to them as you think of more. Say them out loud.

- Write down your areas of weakness. Do not ignore them. Acknowledge them. Especially the areas dealing with self-worth. Can these areas be improved? How?

- Now that you have taken the time to get to know yourself better than any racist ever will, you understand your value. How will this understanding change the way you respond to racist inequalities in your life?

- Spend some time thinking about what you will do or say when you experience or witness racism in real life. Practice what you will say in a mirror. When it happens, you'll be prepared.

NOTES

BAD NEWS

By: Ray Butler

Entrepreneur

What is **Bad News**? **Bad News** is often described as information we avail ourselves to by either, what we hear or see that has a negative impact on our lives. **Bad News** could cause pain, fear, embarrassment, shame, just to name a few affects. Does this cause you to have a flashback? Can you remember a time when you received **Bad News**? Did you react or did you respond? As my grandmother used to say, "you keep living, **Bad News** will come to visit you."

When **Bad News** does travel to you the questions will arise: What shall I do? Whom shall I call, email or text? The pressure is growing, and **Bad News** is still hanging around. I hope to share with you a few ideas that will allow you to face **Bad News** head on and walk away victoriously. I remember distinctly in my teens and mid to late 20's, my solution to **Bad News** was that I would handle it. It did not matter what it was, I was going to handle it. The only challenge was that I had no real valid idea how to manage **Bad News.** I would go at it headfirst often creating a bigger situation. You know what happens when the situation gets bigger or worse, right? We panic! This is never good. A word of caution, "Panic time," means" STOP". Take a deep breath (through the nostrils) exhale slowly (through the mouth). Do this type of breathing for 20 – 30 minutes. These deep breaths will give you an opportunity to think for a moment. To regain control of your emotions. Yes, men have emotions and feelings. Pray to God regarding this matter.

What positive role model, counselor, coach, or adult can you call anytime day or night and share your deepest feelings with? Who will give you solid, sound advice, whether you like it or not, and you respect them for it? This is such a huge thing when **Bad News** arrives. Our world will sometimes get turned upside down. It is always good to have someone to talk to and pray with as we go through these moments.

Once you have regained some stability, you can now begin to process the **Bad News**. What happened? How did it happen? Is this the worst that could happen? What may be the best outcome from this situation? What is the most likely outcome? Please know that sometime **Bad News** is not happening directly to you, but to someone close to you. Therefore, our responses could be different as to how we frame the situation to get it under control in our minds.

CALL TO ACTION:

Remember the question I asked earlier regarding who you could call anytime day or night?

Pause for a moment and go through your contacts and find that person. Call them right now and confirm that they are the person you can count on. Be specific, do not be vague. This is a big ask of someone to commit to you in what may be your darkest moment. Upon confirmation, add this person to your speed dial.

Congratulations… you have made a huge step toward being able to manage **Bad News.**

Bad News sometimes presents a learning or strengthening experience. It could also be a wakeup call or force you to reassess your priorities. Please note over the next few hours, days, months, or years the shock or sting from the **Bad News** will start to soften. However, do not get distracted like I did in my younger years, and rush ahead without staying on course. I was the person that was going to correct the issue without a plan. However, I learned that I must practice self-control and begin to prioritize my thoughts. Sometimes little or no action may be the right option at that time.

Let's recap our options:

A. Stop and breathe 20-30 minutes to regain composer.

B. Pray

C. Dial your confidant (person on your speed dial)

D. Process and frame the matter.

E. Find the learning or strengthening experiences.

F. Practice self-control

G. Prioritize and move forward.

One of the best ways to prepare for **Bad News** is to be a great decision maker. I am going to leave you with a five-day reading plan to help you become a great decision maker.

Read:

Day 1: Nehemiah Chapter 1 verses 1-11.

Decision making is one of the core competencies of being a good Leader. Decisions reveal values and intelligence. They require obedience to and dependence on God. They demand wisdom.

Day 2: Who God is. Genesis Chapter18 verses 18-23.

The God of the Bible is Omniscient, Omnipotent, Omnipresent.

Day 3: Who I am. 1 Chronicles verse 12:32

Good decision making requires adequate information and careful analysis of all the potential facts.

Day 4: How it works. Proverbs Chapter 1 verses 1-6.

Good decisions require accurately processed information. To make good decisions we must attain wisdom and mental discipline to understand words of insight.

Day 5: What I do: Joshua Chapter 9 verses 1-15.

Israel lived with consequences of a decision, that God did not approve. Israel gathered information on a tribe that wanted to create a treaty with them, but (Israel) did not consult God before making the final decision.

As we strive to make good decisions, let's make sure we pray to God for what his will is regarding the matter.

NOTES

DISAPPOINTMENTS

By: Peter Mitchell

Founder of The Rock Medical Service

Weekly Task: Answer who are You? (The Good and Bad) How Do You See Yourself? How do others see You? How do You want People to see You? Topic: Disappointments, how did it make Me feel, and how did I bounce back? Disappointments will come in all shapes, and forms. It can show up in a relationship, or in the form of your favorite sports team losing to your rivals just to name a couple. Mine came in the form of failing Nursing School in the year 2000 and having this ominous cloud hanging over my head until, I realized who was for me, and what my self-worth is.

It was the beginning of a New Millennium, Y2K, year 2000, and I was entering my final semester of Nursing School, prior to this upcoming event. I had never failed at a goal that I set for myself. I am Peter Mitchell, son of Rocky, and Claudette Mitchell, tough, resilient, steadfast, and faith-based parents. Not to mention my sister was one of the first of Black women to graduate from the same Nursing School, and my brother also conquered the same program. Heck, even my mother went through it at the age of 50 plus. So why not me, or so I thought. Well, there was more to that "thought," because up until then I truly believed all I needed to do was play like I was serious about Nursing school. Hey, after all I made it this far. I only had 3 months until I was going to graduate from Nursing school. The funny part is, as the time drew nearer for finals, I started to talk myself out of wanting a Nursing Degree. Do I really know how the heart functions? Do I really understand the Neurological system? Can I truly convert grams to drams? These were some of the questions I could answer with a definite yes, but the point was, I wanted to specialize in Endocrinology Pediatrics. So, when I learned that a mistake in administering medication, the size of a pin head, or the size of the period symbol on your compute could kill a child, I convinced myself that I was not prepared to be a nurse in the real-world environment. This was because I did not put the time into the academics that I claimed to have a passion for.

It was a month prior to finals, while my peers were studying, I was "clubbing," and working at a hospital. I was thinking to myself, oh this is just a game, and I have the answers to master it. The day of finals was here, you could cut the tension, nervousness, and excitement in the air with suture scissors. In the past this nursing program had broken many spirit, and I told myself, "no not me, no matter what the results are I am walking out of here with my head held up high, they won't break Sweet P, Pete Doggy Dog", nicknames that people gave me, and I accepted as a label (mark this). The results were posted, you had to score an 80 to become a new graduate nurse. As they handed my test back to me, I stood there, and looked at the two digits "seven, and an eight. "I scored a 78! I stood there as some screamed from joy, and some from disappointment.

My instructor told me, it's not up to her, but I could talk to the Dean of Nursing, and if they would allow the 2 points, then I would graduate as a nurse. Well, I was one of many that day. I remembered the Dean of Nursing a 5' feet 2 inches African American Woman. I just knew I was going to get those 2 extra points, and as I approached her, and showed my test to her, she spoke these words that I still can hear them clear as a bell. "When does it stop?" I knew exactly what she meant, and what she was saying. Afterall, I was taught by my mother if someone is spelling the word C-A-T, don't let them have to tell you that the word is "Cat" that they are spelling. I told the Dean of Nursing thanks, and walked away never to look back at her, or my peers that were in that class. At that moment I had decided not to go into Nursing feeling a tad relieved, but more so as a Failure. A failure to my family, a failure to my girlfriend, a failure to our son, a failure to the physicians, and nurses I worked with in the operating room that were just as excited for me to become their peer as a Registered Nurse.

Months had passed since I failed Nursing School, the season of the summer was over. Play time was over. No longer was the outside world looking at me as a shining rising star, but now I was just one of many who was a failure. Sweet P, Pete Doggy Dog was mortal! Just another "I'm going to do this, or I'm going to do that" kind of person, earlier I said "mark this" when I gave the nicknames, I was given and accepted. My Father taught me to never let someone put a label on you. If you do then you will always have to agree to it, or always try to debunk it. It was one day I was talking to my loved ones about what happened with nursing school, and as I was trying to cover up the hurt. I was calling myself a failure. That way I could soften the blow if they were going to start to persecute me. But what came out of their mouth in the form of nineteen words changed my life forever to this day. "Peter, you failed, but you are not a failure, you just have to go back to the drawing board"! And just like that the fire restarted in me.

I didn't go back and finish that Nursing degree, but I took everything I learned from that experience and applied it to my life knowing that I am a Child of God, and He did not put me on this earth to be a failure or a piece of garbage. I also knew I didn't want my girlfriend who is now my wife to look at me as if I would be the man that would allow our son to fail, and waddle in a cesspool. I wanted to be my son's superhero. Being poor as a child, and a young man, I knew I had to rise above my self-pity, and look around me and see the support I had in the people who still believed in me and knew I had more to offer than what I was displaying. I knew I had to prove that I am who I always said I was. Peter Mitchell, someone who may need to read instructions 2 or 3 times, someone who was a C student that High School counselors hurried along, but someone who saw greatness when I looked in that mirror. Not because of me, but because God told me that He is King of Kings, and I was created in His image. Yes, my wife was and is the anchor on my ship as well. My siblings heckled me with love to build my tough skin. My parents sent encouragement through scriptures and stories of their past to help me build character.

At some point in our lives, we must know and recognize our own self-worth. We must ask ourselves. "Who am I, the good, and the bad?" And mostly never let someone put a label on you unless you are ready to defend it or dismiss it. Did you know, home runs make up 15.9 percent of the hits in MLB games? This means almost 1 in every 6 hits is a home run. Not every time you step up to bat will you hit a home run, but if you don't swing, then for sure you will never know your potential.

Call To Action:

Set goals, gather the resources, make a plan, and execute it. But if you happen to strike out, be ready to bounce back and swing again. Find a support system, know who you are, and your worth. Know that men died for it, and kids cry for it, and that's for recognition now. To sum up, you are not a failure if you fail, it just means you need to go back to the drawing board. Learn from every disappointment you come across. Surround yourself with people who are for you, not just "get along people," but those who will speak truth into your life. Learn what your self-worth is and do everything in your will to bounce back. Disappointments will come, but from my experiences when I applied these factors into my situation, I was able to bounce back. Before you know it, I am confident that you will too. You'll be hitting life-changing home runs too!

NOTES

HOW A SETBACK SETS UP YOUR COMEBACK

By: Floyd Smith

CEO, Oil & Gas

I have always believed that setbacks are learning opportunities for future comeback successes. I allow myself this position because I accept the fact that I make mistakes and have setbacks. I believe that if I plan to make a move in life or business, I should spend the time evaluating the steps needed for success. However, once I start my plan and my effort fails, creating a setback, I review my steps to figure out what caused the setback. Once I figure out what went wrong to cause the setback, I can take the correct steps in moving forward with my comeback. It is worth saying that very rarely will I discontinue a move after a setback occurs. Because I believe if it was worth doing before the setback; it is still worth doing after making changes to achieve my comeback.

My keys to success are based on two passages of scripture that I love and believe deeply to my soul. The first passage is **Luke 11: 9-10.** In this scripture the Lord says, "**Ask**, and it shall be given you; **Seek**, and you shall find; **Knock**, and it shall be opened unto you. For everyone that **Asketh** receiveth; and he that **Seeketh** findeth; and to him that **Knocketh** it shall be opened." Since the Lord cannot tell a lie; I have always taken him at his word. The other passage supporting this scripture, is **Matthew 6:33** which states, "But **Seek** ye first the kingdom of God, and his righteousness; and All these things shall be added unto you." I believe firmly that if I remain faithful in pursuing Christ's Kingdom, that any life or business opportunities I pursue will be blessed because of the spiritual steps I have stated above. That is why I will Always; Ask; Seek and **Knock**. Being a continual **Kingdom Seeker**, first; God says **"ALL THESE THINGS SHALL BE ADDED UNTO YOU"** which means anything in my life. These passages allow me to live with **POWER** to overcome **SETBACKS** and move ahead for the **COMEBACKS!**

CALL TO ACTION:

Consider my approach to allowing setbacks to setup YOUR comebacks. I charge YOU to be courageous today! Don't YOU ever be afraid of making a mistake today! Remember YOU can only create YOUR successful comebacks, by Seeking the Kingdom of God First! I CHALLENGE YOU to BE a SEEKER!

NOTES

3RD QUARTER

BUILDING

THE IMPORTANCE OF MENTORS

By: James Bradley

Business Owner

A mentor is an experienced and trusted advisor. The role of the mentor is to guide, direct, encourage and hold a mentee (protégé) accountable in areas deemed important for future endeavors. This guidance and direction can cover many areas in the life of the mentee. The title of this chapter assumes the need for mentors. With that fact in mind, one is bound to ask, "why is there a need for mentors?"

When assigned this topic, my original direction was to point out the failings of fathers who are not involved in the lives of their children with the focus on those absentee fathers. After careful consideration of the topic, I conjured up another thought — there is a need for mentors many times even when fathers are involved and present. The role of the father is to provide leadership for the family. A father is to be the provider, protector, and spiritual guide for the family. Most fathers, while doing their best to fulfil these roles, may lack exposure and experience in other areas vital for their children's success. This is where mentors can be important players. If you have a father who is involved in your life, he is your first resource for direction.

What if, however, the direction that you (his son) are interested in pursuing is outside of his expertise? This is where and when a mentor can be important. Careful review of the role of a mentor above should help to make the point. Your father will be able to provide motivation and emotional support, but the rest will fall to the mentor. If you are unclear of which career, your father may be able to assist here because he will know your talents, dreams, and interests. As such, he will be able to help you explore careers. Your father may also aid in setting goals at this phase of your journey. Once you decide your choice of careers, if different than your father's career, it is time to begin your search for a mentor.

Let me see if I can make it real for you! Do you have a little brother or male cousin who looks up to you? Are you able to show him how to do things, how to make things or how to figure out a problem? If so, you mentored him! This is the same concept that you need to employ as you reach the next levels in your growth and maturity. Choosing your mentor will depend on what area you need help in. What I am suggesting is that there is a good chance that you will need more than one mentor.

Consider the different areas of your life that you will encounter. For example, you may have a particular interest in the opposite sex. Oh sure, you may feel that you can handle this on your own. However, as you get older and begin to consider marriage, you may seek a mentor who has a successful, healthy marriage to consult with. When considering your career path, make sure you find someone who can direct you with a choice of schools, courses, and internships. Eventually, you will become interested in your finances. Someone who is successful in all aspects of finance will be invaluable (Get it?). If your family has not instilled in you the value of savings and budgeting, seek this mentor out early—the earlier, the better. This mentor will also be able to advise you on the importance of good credit.

If you are a believer in God, find a spiritual mentor. If you want to thrive in all the aforementioned areas, you really should start with the spiritual mentor. Your spiritual mentor will help put all the other areas— love, career, education, and finance in the proper perspective. Your spiritual mentor will help you avoid the pitfalls of relationships (pregnancies, sex offender charges, STDs, etc. Your spiritual mentor will guide you in putting God first as it relates to possessions, riches, wealth and even popularity. Your spiritual mentor will steer you in the right direction of a career so that you will be able to glorify God and not have to compromise your morals. Speaking of popularity, your spiritual mentor will help you to understand the importance of choosing your friends. The right guidance here could help keep you out of jail, prison, the hospital and even the grave. Your spiritual mentor is the most important mentor to have.

A quick word of caution is in order as well. Be very careful in your selections. It is unfortunate but we live in a time where predators are lurking. Be very selective in your choices! Keep your parents informed of all activities, plans and meetings with your mentor. Good Luck and Blessings to you!

CALL TO ACTION:

I challenge you to make a list of mentors in the different areas mentioned. Seek assistance from those closest to you for ideas. You may even consider multiple mentors for certain areas. I encourage you to begin contacting them for interviews and strategizing with them immediately.

NOTES

BROTHERHOOD

By: David Carter

Government Financial analyst & Retired Army Veteran

Praise God for allowing me a chance to share my thoughts on brotherhood, I am humbled to be asked by a great man to express my views on the topic. Vine's Expository Dictionary of New Testament Words defines brotherhood as.

Brother, Brethren, Brotherhood, Brotherly:

denotes "a brother, or near kinsman;" in the plural, "a community based on identity of origin or life." It is used of:

(1) male children of the same parents, **Matt 1:2; 14:3;**

(2) male descendants of the same parents, **Act 7:23, 26; Hbr 7:5;**

(3) male children of the same mother, **Mat 13:55; 1Cr 9:5; Gal 1:19;**

(4) people of the same nationality, **Act 3:17, 22; Rom 9:3.** With "men" (aner, "male"), prefixed, it is used in addresses only, **Act 2:29, 37, etc.;**

(5) any man, a neighbor, **Luk 10:29; Mat 5:22; 7:3;**

(6) persons united by a common interest, **Mat 5:47;**

(7) persons united by a common calling, **Rev 22:9;**

To this dialogue I would like to focus on definition #7. I would encourage you to align yourself with people with a common positive calling, surround yourself with folks that are more experienced than you in a given topic and share your knowledge. Looking back throughout my life, I found myself wanting to be in the company of people I felt were smarter than me. Now why did I do this? As I am self-reflecting, I am understanding there is a little hidden piece of me that wants to always learn, be smarter and use that knowledge to help other people, a brotherhood.

Being in the Army for over 20 years taught me many life lessons, but I will focus on the brotherhood aspect. Brotherhood for me means any brother can come from any background. When in a foxhole I can only point my weapon in one direction at any given time, my brothers can only point their weapons in one direction at a time, and we must all cover our sectors of fire to save our lives. Now in this foxhole everyone is not from the same block, city, state or even country at times, but we must all trust our brother to have our back! So, I encourage you to have your brothers back.

Find a brother that will mentor you. Mark Victor said "Each one, reach one. Each one, teach one. Until all are taught." A mentor should be able to give you guidance for life, share their experiences to make you better. These shared life events will help you throughout your life. Get a mentor that will show you how to prepare for an interview, buy a home, how to interact with the police, how to stand up for social injustice in a way it will be well received. Be open to that mentor, be vulnerable and open to criticism. Remember that brother wants to help, and the critique is to make you better even when you do not want to hear it. Once you have experienced similar life events, share that knowledge until all your brothers are taught.

CALL TO ACTION:

I charge you from this moment forward to be part of a brotherhood. Find a group of brothers with Godly positive common life goals, brothers who are seeking growth and knowledge, and brothers who want to see you succeed. Seek that life mentor, be open and willing to learn from them, be receptive to their advice and critique. Also, be a great brother to the brotherhood, have your brother's back, and teach one!

NOTES

CHANGING GEARS

By: Jeremy Black

Real Estate/Technology Entrepreneur CEO of Akilieum Investmenst, LLC

Ten seconds on the shot clock. The ball is in your hands. You call for a pick and roll. Your two-guard comes to the top of the three-point-line to set a screen. Seven seconds. Your two-guard's defender comes along, forming a cluster of trouble getting to the rim. Five seconds. Quickly thinking, you spin off your defender and go straight to the rim. Four seconds. The score was 77-76. Down by just a basket, you know that a layup, or a possible foul could win you the game. Three seconds. A four-guard is down on the block, hindering you from reaching the goal. Two seconds. "Body up the big man to draw a foul," you think to yourself, even though there is an open teammate at the three-point line. Bumping into the defender, you carefully shoot the ball toward the net. Game Over.

Life is full of choices that need to be made. As we begin this new, unprecedented era of uncertainty, it is now more imperative than ever that we learn to change gears, pivot, change directions, take another route. Why? The answer is simple: The choices you make today will affect your tomorrow.

My name is Jeremy Black, and I own a successful real estate investment company, Akilieum Investments LLC, as well as a development software engineer. To some people, I am successful, but I remain humble for a few reasons. First, I was not always in the position I am in now. Second, where I am today is a direct result of hard work, intense study and KNOWING WHEN TO CHANGE GEARS. Prior to my current position, I was working at a fast-food restaurant 50+ hours a week for $11.50 an hour. I knew that this job was not going to bring me wealth or happiness, and so one day after being "sick and tired of being sick and tired," I quit my job and started studying to learn how to code. Sometimes, when you are trying to get where you are wanting to go, you must drop everything holding you back, and just go after what you want. I then found out how to buy and sell real estate without using any of my own money (wholesaling) and found myself receiving a $11,000 check for selling a property. I knew a had made a change for the better.

Changing gears first requires you to assess your current situation. As young men, you have your whole life ahead of you to make mistakes and learn from them. But as someone who has been in your shoes, I want to try to help you skip some of the hardships you may face later in your lives. Assessing your situation means looking at where you are currently in your life, and then carefully map out a path to success. Are you not happy with where your life is currently going? It is never too late to dig deep and go after what you really want. Do you want to be a doctor? This requires intense study of the human body and much dedication. Want to be the next CEO of a major tech company like Google or Apple? Start to learn how to code now.

If none of my co-author's addressed this, I want to make sure you are all equipped with the tools necessary to make the best decisions in life. Many of these tips have been withheld from the black community for centuries by those who wish to see us fail as a race.

Credit: The saying, "Cash is king" is true, but credit makes the world go around. Forget everything you have learned about credit being bad and start training your mind to think like the wealthy. As soon as you obtain your very first credit card, your credit score will be used to obtain cars, houses, and the best of what life has to offer. Just remember a few things about credit and things will go well for you. 1) Always keep your balance under thirty percent of what your credit limit is. 2) Always, pay your bill on time, no matter what. 3) Never borrow what you cannot pay back.

Saving: I was told that the audience I was to write to was 13-17-year-old young men. Assuming that if you are old enough to have a job, that you are working to provide some income to buy the latest shoes, clothes, jewelry, and to go on dates. That is great, but please remember to save some of your money for a rainy day. I recommend that for every paycheck you receive, that you save thirty percent (e.g., saving thirty dollars for every one hundred dollars you save).

Investing: With the help of your parent or guardian, open a Roth IRA or invest in stocks. No, you are not too young to do these things. No, it is not complicated. There are plenty of 13-year-olds investing in the stock market; and in 2020, we are in the age of technology and information, so this information is readily available on Google and YouTube. Believe me when I say this: At the time of writing this chapter, I am 26 years old, and if I had known any of this information when I was 13 and acted on it, I would have been a millionaire by the time I was 18.

CALL TO ACTION:

You may think you are stuck in your current situation or may find yourself like this in the future. But you are young, with plenty of time to explore your interests, so do not think where you are now will be your final destination. Read, observe, and learn as much as you can to be able to change when times get rough.

I want to leave you with some parting words of wisdom. There are very few things in life that are worth your time and energy. Money, cars, fame, status, clothes, jewelry, being "that guy" are not among them. Providing for your family, creating generational wealth, passing down assets, and having your family name live on past your lifetime are some of the most rewarding and worthwhile endeavors one can take in this life. I wish you the best and I wish you well.

NOTES

ENCOURAGEMENT

By: Luis Avila

General Manager

My young brother, my friend, today I write to you to tell you of my thoughts about these days of Covid 19, the world we are living in, the challenges that may lie ahead and to encourage you to always look at the positive side of things as hard as it may sometimes seem. First, let me tell you a little bit about myself. I am a 52-year-old Hispanic male, son of amazing parents who this week celebrated 55 years of marriage. I have an older sister, younger sister, and younger brother. I have been married 20 years to my beautiful wife and have a beautiful daughter who is a successful writer and professor living in Boston Ma. Believe me, I am not an expert in anything, but in my 52 years of life I have experienced many wonderful things as well as challenges.

Now, let me take you several decades back to when I was a young teenage lad, full of life with not a care in a world except playing sports, eating, watching tv and enjoying my friends and wonderful family. I was blessed to be raised with loving, caring parents who always encouraged me to do the best that I could at everything I set my mind out to do. Unfortunately, sometimes it took more than encouragement on their part to get through my head all the good things they wanted for me. Temptation to do the easy thing or the fun thing in life was and is always there no matter what age you may be. I made mistakes along the way but fortunately God and sometimes luck got me through the turbulent times. Gangs, bullying, drugs and temptation were always and will always be out there lingering in our lives.

Fortunately, my faith in God and my mom and dad's voice is always in my head saying "mijo" (son) remember, we won't always be there to watch you and to encourage you to do the right thing… but God, who loves you as much as we do will always be there to guide you in the right path. My parents always had a very strong faith, attending church regularly and very involved in church groups. Some of their closest friends were priests, nuns or those close to the church. My dad even attended a seminary at the age of 14 with dreams of being a priest someday. Although his faith remained, he became homesick and later returned home and pursued the navy.

I would love to say that my faith was as strong as theirs at that age, however, when I was that age, I had many other interests. I did appreciate and take in all their teachings though. I prayed every night. What I mostly prayed to God for is to not let my parents die until I was at least 25 years of age. My age of 25 has now doubled, and I am now 52. I am selfish in asking God to please leave my parents here with me on earth for several more years. Fast forward to 2020. What a challenging, difficult scary time we are living in.

Covid 19 life: Believe me, this virus is scary as heck, not just for me but knowing how harmful it can be for my elderly parents. When this virus first started, I did not really understand it. Today is June 24 and I have not worked for 3 months because of the virus. Knowing now what I know, if I could, I would go back in time and encourage my teenage self to not only look at how boring life has been because I could not hang out with friends, go to the movies, go out to eat or even play the game of baseball that I love. I would ask my teenage self to look at this wonderful time and create memories with the ones you love because one day they may be gone.

Black Lives Matter protests: Again, I am not an expert on anything, and I am blessed to have lived a very sheltered life in my Hispanic community. However, if I could go back and talk to my younger self, I would encourage myself to take it all in with open eyes and an open heart and to process, listen, speak, and act positively and without hurting myself, my parents, humankind and especially my God through my thoughts, words, or actions.

CALL TO ACTION:

My young brother, my friend, today, I encourage you to think about who you are, who you want to be, who you want to talk to and ask for strength, guidance encouragement or to just vent frustration. What are your dreams? How will you accomplish those dreams? Today, I encourage you to be caring, faithful, thoughtful, respectful, joyful but most of all Love. Love yourself.

NOTES

FROM 1G TO 5G: FROM A BLACK PERSPECTIVE

By: Richard D Moore III

Wireless Telecom Technical Service Lead Owner of WRS

I want to start this by saying thank you to all the people who are going to read this. I want you to understand that, amongst all things, this is a lesson that was taught to me. It basically took about 30 years of my life, and I am going to attempt to condense it down in a chapter. I want to thank God for allowing me to have the opportunity to learn from my mistakes and still overcome them. It is not a very pleasant story, unfortunately. The good news is that most fairy tales do have a happy ending. With that said, we'll go ahead and get started. The comparison that I am giving you all in this story, is a comparison in decades. Decades of my life and decades of the evolution of cellular technology. It is funny in a sense that somehow these things relate to each other for me as you continue to read. I guess I must relate back to when I was just 18 years old and struggling. I had basically made it to my senior year in high school and decided that the streets were a better opportunity for me than completing my high school education. So, I dropped out of school during my senior year.

Keep in mind, this is back in 1988 and like the Black Lives Matter movement that's going on currently today in 2020. Back in 1988 there was a revolution for blacks to return to Africa. The problem was, Africa did not want us back! In turn, we still represented the back to Africa movement. We wore African symbols and attire. The red, black, and green, and I'm not talking about Gucci. Black Power was the movement and we fought against oppressions that were going on with minimum wages and the jobs that they were offering. I decided that the streets and the drugs might produce a bit more wealth, and it did. In three years, I had become one of the higher paid dealers that was around and unfortunately, that ended in a prison term. So that did not turn out well. I had a friend that I grew up with and we were doing business together, but unfortunately, he ended up getting on the drugs. He then turned state evidence against me, and he also testified against me in court (sometimes referred to as snitching).

The outcome was that God had blessed me, and I only ended up doing about four months in prison. The problem with going to prison is that the case followed me for the next 30 years of my life. During that time the 1G and 2G were just starting. That is the second generation of cell phones. We had beepers and a few privileged people did have cell phones. This turned into a business venture. I was selling cell phone chips in the neighborhood. For the people who had phone cells. We were charging about 150 dollars a month to re-chip the cell phones. Back then, technology was awfully slow. There was obviously no video, and you could not send a page with your cell phone. At that time, you had to send a page from a home phone or payphone to text a pager. The pagers were a part of the second generation of technology. We utilized that technology to the fullest, freeing us from standing on the street corners.

What do you do to keep from being arrested? I will say that in 1988, Ronald Reagan declared the war on drugs. The police officer's chose to take that time to round every black male up and give them a case, whether you were innocent or guilty. It was almost systematical racism. When Reagan declared war on drugs, he declared war on the black community. The neighborhoods were policed heavily. If the police even seen you, you better take off running because they were coming for you with absolutely no cause. Later in the 90s the laws were changed to justify the unlawful practices that were going on in the 80s.

I want to let you know; we have always been proud people. We have always stood up for our rights, and equality. You must understand that this battle has been going on for centuries. Let's look at a number one example, if we just take you back a few decades to the 60s. The police and the white community were still using basically slavery tactics, dogs, and water hoses to try to control us. We did learn something back then. We learned that you must work hard. We learned that you must be organized. We learned that if you do not do it for yourself, nobody is going to do it for you. We saw communities' flourish. Everybody in every neighborhood knew each other. Everybody in each hood helped each other.

As I fast forward a few years to the mid-90s, at that time I was around 25 years old. I do believe that most people, at least males at that age, will have some changes. From a teenage or adolescent mind set to someone that thinks before they act. I had a person in my life that really meant a lot to me. He was my mentor, and he was my grandfather. I was the age of 10 during the time he had a business named Gantt's Radio and TV Repair. This was when there were tube TVs, and we would test tubes and transformers. It was a completely different era, tube TVs versus the electronics and semiconductor technology that we have now. I would work with him on the weekends. As I grew up, I always worked with him and learned electronics. Now, mind you, I did not realize at that time that I was learning a trade that would ultimately transform my life in my later years.

By the late 90s, we ended up with the third generation of cell phones. (UMTS is the term that we used) I decided to leave Michigan and move to Texas, where I began working with the company Nokia. Back then, I was just a warehouse worker. I was tested and the knowledge that my grandfather gave me about electronics landed me a job as OJT, so I ended up getting a trainer position. I wasn't making much but moved up rapidly within that company and I learned a new trade. It was called IT radio base station or BTS systems. What these systems do is, they are the communication piece, or the network that allows the cell towers to transmit a signal and propagate from tower to tower also to the EU or cell phone. So that's kind of how cell phones work. 3G brought phones to parents and mobilize business, still no video. Information wasn't traveling but 1 mega bps.

Wow time has passed, and LTE or 4G technology has come and evolved. Long Term Evolution (LTE), and what an evolution it's been. The video was in here and the money came marching in! The year was 2012 and WRS is on the scene, no longer an employee but an employer. WRS is a small but experienced telecom company and 4G was our thing. Just as I evolved to WRS, 4G evolved to 5G with speeds up to 1gig bit per second. The world is yours for the taking. I challenge you to learn the technologies that will change the world. Your Tik/Toc and Zoom are using this technology, where cars drive with only one passenger in them. Machine to Machine communication allows trackers to farm the land with no driver and yes VR or Virtual Remote where Doctors do surgery remotely with a robot.

This is the future you inherited so take advantage of it. Life is about you, and what you choose to do. You must remember that if you don't strive and believe in yourself, no one is going to believe in you. How you handle yourself at a noticeably young age will automatically reflect on how you end up living your life when you're older. Concentrate on your future. You can't worry about if you've been mistreated. You must shake it off. Stay focused and if you can have a relationship with yourself, and love yourself, then the sky's the limit for you! Be a leader. Do things that no one thinks that you can accomplish. Instill in your heart you know you can do it. This kind of hard work always pays off. No one's going to give it to you. Take it, you must have a mindset that everything you want, you are going to get it.

As we look back at what happened and the reason why I say the case followed me for 30 years, is every time I filled out a job application later in my life, there was a question on it. Have you ever been convicted of a felony? And every time, even to this day when I see that question, I must stop and think about if I am going to check, yes.

In conclusion. I just want to say one more thing to all of you. I must tell you about one of my favorite characters. It is a Warner brother cartoon. Pinky and the brain. You may not have heard of it but yeah you can look it up on YouTube. Because every single night this little lab rat comes up with a plan to take over the world. Then every morning he's back in the cage. That is OK because once he gets some sleep, he is going to come up with another plan to take over the world the next night. Take that never giving up concept and you will succeed. There is no way that you can fail.

CALL TO ACTION:

Be respectful and mindful of others. That is how you make it. Because at the end of the day. You can look yourself in the mirror and say, "I gave 100 percent!" Even if you do not see these materialistic things that you want now, Guess what? You will see them in the coming future. Have a blessed future.

NOTES

THE IMPORTANCE OF READING

By: J.R. Moore III

High School English Teacher

As an English teacher, I have been advocating for my students to spend more time reading good books for years. I strive to be encouraging, and I try to help them select texts that will hold their interest. I even let them take my personal copies home with them in the hope that they will begin reading the book and be mesmerized by its content. Sometimes I am pleasantly surprised when they come back and want to talk about what they have read, but often, they tell me that they didn't really like it. That can be a demoralizing feeling. I sometimes become disheartened when I hear them say things like, "I don't like reading," or "I haven't read a book since the sixth grade". My reply to such statements is always direct. It is also meant to cut deep to the root cause of the statement. I simply ask, "Are you proud of that?" If you like to read, GREAT! I'm extremely proud of you.

I suspect that most young people who read this book will more than likely be in the same boat as my students. So, I now pose this same question to you, the reader of this book, who I assume must have some comfortability with reading. The question now, however, has an upgraded meaning. Since you obviously read, the question now encapsulates additional questions for you to respond to internally. Those questions include: When was the last time you read to educate yourself? How often do you read to understand history? Do you read only to bolster what you already believe? How often do you read something that makes you truly uncomfortable? Now, with the knowledge of these adjoining questions, I ask "Are you proud of that?" Are you proud of your lack of awareness? Are you proud of your one-dimensional view of the world? Are you proud of the fact that you have not pushed yourself beyond your comfort zone? Are you proud of that?

You see, when you read books, you give yourself a chance to grow. You get to grow in your understanding of issues that affect you personally as well as issues that you can only imagine. You get to see what life is like in circumstances that you will never find yourself a part of. This is a marvelous gift and a tremendous opportunity! This is the only medium where you can get an in-depth understanding of someone else's life. Movies can only give you a glimpse into a character's motives, thoughts, and feelings. After all, they typically last about two hours. How well can you know someone after only two hours? Books, on the other hand, allow you the time and the necessary explanations to truly know each person and event that you read about. Whether they are fiction or nonfiction, books can transport you into places you have never even heard of and allow you to experience things that you otherwise would not be able to. As young men, you will never have the first-hand knowledge of what it feels like to be a young girl hiding from Nazi soldiers in the middle of your adolescence. Likewise, you will never know the terror of running away from a slave plantation knowing that if you are caught, you will most likely be tortured, mutilated, and possibly killed to set an example for other slaves who may be thinking of running away. Luckily for us, Anne Frank kept a diary and Frederick Douglass wrote in explicit detail. So, although we will never live it, through their words, we can feel their experiences. Reading the words of others connect us in ways that cannot be quantified.

Books are also important to us because they help us to understand the past as a way to plan and prepare for the future. They warn us of things that could happen if we repeat the mistakes of those who came before us. They teach us lessons that we can read about, free us of consequences, rather than experiencing them ourselves. The knowledge that we gain from these books can be vital to our lives. How blessed we are to have the chance to learn from the successes and failures of others. By reading about what has worked for others and what pitfalls they faced, we essentially have access to a playbook that can guide us as we strive to learn and reach our goals.

Therefore, I encourage you to read to empower yourself. Learn all that you can to put yourself in a position to win. A popular saying for the lottery used to be, "You can't win if you don't play." Of course, this is true, but I believe there is another truth that is even more important. **YOU CAN'T WIN IF YOU DON'T KNOW THE RULES.** One of my favorite things to read is my copy of the Constitution of the United States. This may sound strange to some, but I assure you that it has been helpful for me. I tell my students to add it to their reading lists, and you should do the same. The logic behind this is simple. We are governed by the words in that document. The laws that protect or condemn us all start there. And I'm a firm believer that you cannot win a game if you don't know the rules. This is what I mean when I say, "Read to empower yourself. Read things that matter; things that challenge you and make you stretch. Read things that help you to improve your understanding of the world and yourself." Once you start, you will never want to return to the way things were before.

CALL TO ACTION:

Take action by finding one book to read that will entertain you. Then find a book to read that will educate you on a specific subject. This could be a historically relevant text or simply a book that covers a subject that you are interested in learning more about. Lastly, find a book to read that challenges you to do something. The options on each subject are vast and varied. There is something for everyone between the pages of the right book. What are you waiting for? Start reading!

NOTES

READING IS FUNDAMENTAL

By: Terrence Washington

Retired Air Force Veteran

The saying "reading is fundamental" is a very true statement. It is a necessary core for everyday living. Getting from one place to another, choosing the right product, or just catching up on current events are all ways in which the ability to read keeps us moving. But reading is so much more than that.

There is great power in reading a good book because the simple act of reading has benefits both seen and unseen. Regardless of which genre you choose to explore, prepare to lose yourself within the pages of your selection. Reading a good book can have so many positive effects on you physically as well as mentally. Let's discuss some genres.

Fiction, or books that are not based on truth, are usually a fan favorite. Visiting faraway places of the past, delving into a futuristic quest, or finding oneself in a world of total make-believe, only scratches the surface of where fiction books can take you. Books of this type include classic literature, short stories, plays, horror/sci-fi, and even graphic novels just to name a few. Fiction books tend to excite, relax, or entertain a person.

Now non-fiction books (which are based on truth) can be excellent reads in which to get lost. This genre includes biographical books (written based on someone else's account, research, or interviews) and autobiographical books (written by the subject of the book). When you sit down to read these books, expect to learn about people, places, and things. You will become immersed in your favorite sports figures, political leaders, celebrities, etc. These writings can motivate and inspire, raise awareness and consciousness, or simply give a view of how others live or lived.

Historical books just recount information that has happened within the realms of history. This genre is closely related to biographies because some history sometimes discusses a person in history. For example, a person might read about our prehistoric past, events that occurred during times of war, or the history of one's state of birth. This may sound like that textbook that you hate to tackle, but at least if you choose a book of this writing style you can pick exactly what you want to know about!

With inspirational books, the goal of the author is to motivate an individual in spiritual ways. These books can be biographical/autobiographical or non-fiction. Usually someone triumphs over a devastating existence through spiritual growth and redemption. This could include stories of the Bible or uncomplicated stories that lead to God.

If you have a desire to learn about other places, then travel books are for you. Oftentimes these books exhibit chapters filled with colorful pages of scenery and the indigenous people who live there. The words layout just as colorful detailed information about the history and culture. Let your imagination dine on exotic foods, participate in local customs and events, and expand your knowledge outside of your existence and become a world traveler!

Self-help books instruct the reader on solving problems. Books in this genre allow the reader to learn about themselves or others and can equip them with strategies to address the issue at hand. Self-help books can also help an individual unlock hidden talents or perhaps develop the talents they desire. Books about personality, mental illness, and problems are but a drop in the bucket of what you might find here.

As this world becomes less and less predictable, frustration and anxiety can make it hard to know where to turn. Well, reading a good book can be a great way to help relieve and manage stress. Research has even shown that that reading helps stimulate our brains; thereby, lessening the chance of getting Alzheimer's disease or dementia. The genres discussed only cover a small fraction of what is out there. Books on business, art, nutrition, the list goes on and on. Books transport us to other times and places and allow us to connect with other people, times, and places. Most of all they allow us to connect with ourselves.

CALL TO ACTION:

Slough off the day, grab that book you have been eyeing, put the "real world" on the shelf, and escape!

NOTES

READ! THE POWER OF THE PEN

By: Jalen Christopher

College Student

Isn't it funny that the best advice is given as a child? Treat people the way you want to be treated. Share with others. Tell the truth. The one I wanted to focus on is to read books. Books are to the mind what training is to a fighter. Books put the mind in an environment where it will become stronger, faster, and better than before. You may say, "yeah yeah, I've heard that before, so what? Reading books doesn't do anything useful." To that I would say, give me a little bit of your time and I will show you just a few of the many practical and convenient advantages of reading.

Reading books translates into being a better speaker, being a more interesting individual, and discovering new opportunities. Reading out loud could be the difference between you and the thing you desire. Have you ever noticed that the most important people always speak? The boss will give a pep talk at work. The principal will speak at the school assembly. The president will make an address when something happens in the country. In sports, the commentators make as much money as the players, and at the end of the game the only people that get interviewed are the star players.

Public speaking is an indispensable tool and can make the difference between a great associate and a great boss. So, what does this have to do with reading aloud? By reading out loud the reader learns how to breathe, take pauses, and bring a story to life. Reading out loud teaches the reader rhythm, inflection, and showmanship. We have all had a conversation where we ramble, mix up our words, or feel like we are being boring. Reading out loud fixes that problem by making it a habit to give natural pauses and bring life into words. So, the next time you are thinking about talking to the person you like or someone you want to impress, read a little and then go for it. Now that you can talk without rambling through your words, it is time to give you interesting material to talk about.

Reading interesting material makes for intriguing conversation. If you do not travel the world or you're not a celebrity, it can feel like your life is boring and thus what you can talk about is boring too. Author and photographer, Zero Dean said, "If you are bored, you are boring. "He goes on to point out that there are so many things in the world to do. That it is up to you to pick one. With books you can have any adventure you want, and you can have it in the comfort of your home. Not only that, when you are talking to someone at a work function or family gathering you can naturally bring up interesting things. All you have to say is, "I was reading this article..." and go on to talk about what sparked your curiosity. This ability paired with your speaking skills to bring your words to life will capture your audience and want them to know more. When you can speak with confidence, and you have something interesting to say, the only thing left is to do something new with your newfound knowledge.

Reading unlocks doors of the world that you didn't know existed. To put it simply, you don't know what you don't know. When you read, you start to crack open doors to the unknown. The best part, once the door is open, the world around you starts to change with this new information. It is like when you meet a coworker or classmate for the first time. Now, it seems that you see that person all the time, whereas before, you did not see them at all. This means that now what you want and care about are seemingly at your fingertips. Want to buy a house for much less than market value? There is a book for that. Want to try to be a good role model for your kids and family? There is a book for that. Want to have the lifestyle where you never have to worry about money again? Say it with me, there is a book for that. Not only will the books give you instructions on the how, but also on the who. This way you can follow your favorite business tycoon and see the steps they took to get what you want. When it comes down to it, this is all about developing who you are to get what you want. The question is, are you ready for the adventure?

When you discover something new it is a wonderful feeling. However, discovering new depths of something old is life changing. It's like watching a movie you have seen before but laughing at a joke or reference you just now know about. Reading has so many layers, each with its own advantages. Reading out loud allows you to be an effective communicator. Reading intriguing material makes you an intriguing person. Finally, reading can allow you to discover new opportunities. What makes those old rules in kindergarten so special is that they are simple, they are straight forward, and they can set you up for success. The big promotion, being surrounded by people that want to be near you, and new opportunities are all just a couple of books away.

CALL TO ACTION:

Get a book (hardcover or electronic) and read it out loud. Set a time in the day to this consistently for an easily doable amount of time. This could mean reading for 3 minutes, this could mean reading for 30 minutes. The point is to do this every day. If after your set time is up, you want to keep reading, then keep reading. The point is to make reading so easy that there is no reason for you not to read. Commit to reading for 3 weeks and I promise you will see a difference.

NOTES

BOOKS: THE SECRET KEY TO WEALTH AND SUCCESS

By: Jeremy Black

Real Estate Technology Entrepreneur

As I have mentioned multiple times in this book, educating yourself will lead you to information across many subjects from finance to law, real estate to medicine and much more. Books give you access to other people's lives, and by reading about their life, not only will you learn what pitfalls to avoid, but also what shortcuts to take. For this chapter, I'll be discussing some recent and favorite books and some major lessons that I have taken from them.

"Never Split the Difference" is a book by Chris Voss, a former FBI Hostage Negotiator. I have used this book to strengthen my negotiation skills and tactics when negotiating for a raise, job promotion, acquiring real estate at my desired price, and dealing with difficult people in my everyday life.

This book is basically a training manual on how to get what you want, while growing confidence in yourself. This book gives multiple scenarios, such as negotiating a hostages' release, and buying a new car, and the template of what to say during each conversation to achieve the best outcome. This book has taught me that everything is negotiable, and nothing is ever set in stone. I bet some of these conversation templates could be used on your parents to buy you that new PlayStation 5, or new pair of Yeezys or Jordans!

The next book, "The Pact" by Drs. Sampson Davis, George Jenkins, Rameck Hunt, is about three young men who made a pact to become doctors. This book is important to me because it is a reminder that we cannot do everything alone. Sometimes we need a support system to keep us accountable, and to push us to be the very best that we can be. No matter where our lives may have started out, you can still make something great of yourself. Even if you grew up with no father or mother, in a bad neighborhood, living in public housing, wearing hand-me-downs or clothes from a secondhand store, find the people that want to make positive change in their life and become friends with them. Push each other past your limits and never give up on your dreams.

As a child, I was gifted with a 'Lateral Thinking Puzzles book. This book is not a novel about someone's life, rather a book filled with word problems that forced me to think outside the box. I believe that this book has contributed to my incredible skill of looking at a problem, not being discouraged by it, and coming up with a solution that others may not have thought of. Sometimes (if not many) in life you will face what seems to be an insurmountable obstacle, with no clear way through or around it. But don't panic! The greatest triumphs in history came from those who were brave enough to take on a problem, no matter how far out of reach the solution seemed.

CALL TO ACTION:

The power of reading good books filled with information and puzzles to work out your brain will come in handy as you come across situations in life that call for one to take charge and tackle the problem head on. By you being that person, that leader, others will want to follow you, and you never know where that will take you.

NOTES

"ENLARGE MY TERRITORY: 1 CHRONICLES 4: 9,10"

By: Chris Mitchell

Minister

As I was thinking about what to write as an encouragement to young men, I couldn't help but think back to my younger days. Yeah, yeah … I know that was a while ago, but still a journey worth taking. What I used as a "mental roadmap" was just a question. Simply enough, "what do I wish I would've been told?" What I know now is that there are no "do-overs." Sometimes teenage decisions last well into manhood and sometimes to the grave. Whatever was happening then did not have to warp and distort my future in a permanent way.

I just wished that someone would've taught me about a little-known Bible character by the name of Jabez. See, I identify with this cat. He wasn't given a silver-spoon at birth (neither did I growing up in Pleasant Grove), he was trying to be a decent dude, probably wasn't well liked by his siblings, and the icing on the cake seems that his mama only saw him as a pain, hence the meaning of the name Jabez. Despite all the potential setbacks and possible excuses, he asked God for three things. And guess what, God gave him all three! Before I get to the part where I say, "and you can ask Him for the same things (well I guess I just did)," let's look at what he asked for.

The first thing Jabez asked for was *more* responsibility. I know that most translations say that he asked for a larger territory, but you cannot have more territory without it bringing more responsibility with it. It's an accepted fact that the responsibilities you have as a teenager prepare you for greater responsibilities later as an adult. How does school, chores, and having a part-time job lead to an "enlarged territory?" It develops a good work ethic!

One of the biggest challenges I've had in my adult life is having a good, consistent work ethic. I get the job done but not always to the best of my ability. I was more concerned with saying I was finished than I was with saying it was my best. If you're able to set this in place now at your age, imagine all that God will place into your custody (Luke 12:48).

The next thing he asked God for was that God would hold his hand. Again, this is realized by word analysis, but this is the essence of the request that God's hand would be with him. I knew as a teenager how important it was to hold to God's unchanging hand (did you start singing?). I mean they drilled it into my head every Sunday and every Wednesday. And I tried! But there was a problem!

The problem was I kept trying to take Him to places I wanted to go. They were places that no one wanted to hear about God. I shouldn't have been there, and I shouldn't have tried to take God there. See, Jabez asked to hold God's hand which means that God is doing the leading. He asked God to take him where God wanted him to be. I'm sitting here thinking right now of how much time I've lost because I had to learn the value of His leadership. Good news for you is you can get it now!

The third thing Jabez asked for really resonates with me. It has to do with pain. He asked God to keep him from hurt and harm. Life can be full of pain. So many people are living through pain because they've been hurt and harmed. There are some pains that must be experienced, but there are others that God can keep away.

CALL TO ACTION:

Jabez simply asks that whatever hurt and harm that can be avoided that God not let him experience it. What a request. In a world where fame and fortune are on the menu of most people, little do they realize that Mo' money Mo' problems (probably just showed how old I am). What I'm driving at is developing the ability to trust God to the point of missing a lot of the hurt and harm that some decisions bring.

Enough of the sermon stuff. I've taken a page out of Jabez' playbook. I'm running a little behind schedule, but I'm on God's time now. I've asked God for these same three things. I'm like, "hey, if Jabez could have them so can I!" And if I can have them, so can you!

NOTES

FINANCIAL POWER

By: Derrick Johnson

Engineer, Entrepreneur

Today in society money is important, it is very crucial to the fabric of American society. However, as significant as money is in our culture, it is not taught in most schools today. Financial literacy is singularly one of the greatest traits to have when entering adulthood. Financial power is monetarily creating impact or change in an economic environment.

Learning how to (1) make money, (2) invest money, and (3) spend monies will thrust one into another tier of societal standards. Making money is a fundamental step on the road to financial power. The common ways to make money are by obtaining a job or starting a company that increases purchasing power. Purchasing power is the value of how many products and goods can be bought with a currency.

Earning money is focal to building financial power. When money is made, it is common to save money and store it for hard times. The minute money is made, one has to learn how to store it. Essential means to life are food, water, and shelter. After these necessities are accounted for, only then can one begin to save capital. Four months of essential means should be stored to account for the unknown future. Financial discipline needs to be practiced by not purchasing items/goods of no value. In laymen's terms, assets make money, and liabilities do not make money while costing you money. Nevertheless, this is a financial wealth building mindset, hence, saving money is a strategy for investing currency to double the value of it.

Investing is defined as spending money in a venture with the expectation of achieving a profit. Investing will always be required for financial power. The instant money is saved, it should be invested to make the money work for more money and not leave money stored. There are a few investment wealth vehicles that are proven to be fail proof throughout time. Think about this, most individuals will always need food (restaurants, food trucks etc.), shelter (real estate), and medical attention (medical technologies). Investing in ventures that align with these categories will always be frugal for doubling money.

Spending money (financial discipline) is the utmost key to financial power. Spending habits of a people define the beginning of wealth or the destruction of wealth. Buying liabilities prevents the flow of money, cutting down financial power and influence in a culture. Nice cars, clothes, and big houses (with a mortgage) are a great look if your financial literacy choices have enabled you to be comfortable while still saving to maintain these liabilities. Purchasing life insurance before care insurance is a great way of spending/investing money to secure more wealth.

CALL TO ACTION:

In closing, the right combination of these habits and knowledge will breed financial power. Financial power speaks volumes to civilizations. It takes money to build communities, run organizations, produce healthy foods, etc. Becoming financially empowered leads families to prominence and future wealth for generations to build upon and enjoy.

NOTES

MONEY SAVING INVESTING

By: Ernie D. Seay

Owner of Run Your Dreams

My brother was 11 and I was 10 years old when we got our first job. We delivered papers in the neighborhood. We had a lot of people on our paper route. We grew up in Michigan so in the wintertime, it got really cold. I'm so glad we started in the summer because by the time winter came, we knew and understood what it would take to finish the route in a timely manner. We would have to go pick up the papers, bring them home, fold them, put them in our satchels and deliver them to hundreds of houses all before a certain time. On Friday's we would collect the money for the papers from each of the customers that we delivered to. After collecting the money, we would have to pay for all the papers we delivered for the week. After all the papers were paid for, we were able to keep the profits. This was one of the best jobs to have as a kid. We spent some, saved some, gave some away to help a friend or two but at the end of the day, we were able to work and have money in our pockets at a very young age.

Today, there are so many ways to make money. There are legal ways and illegal ways. I want to make sure we keep it as real as possible. Just understand, there are repercussions and consequences of illegal actions. That's not what we are doing. That's not the road we are taking. Circumstances may have you leaning in that direction but rest assured, there are other ways to make money.

Do your research, and you can start your own business. You can write books, create a tutorial, build something with your hands and sell it, tutor other students, work for someone in the family. The list is endless if you really look to find creative ways to make money. It may be a challenge to work, go to school, do your chores (no complaining about this), participate in extra-curricular activities and all the other things that come your way, but it is possible to do.

Saving is critical. Spending everything you make doesn't make a lot of sense now does it. Only to have to do it all over again. If you're living at home (as I'm sure most of you are) then your output (bills) should be at an all-time low. You probably don't have a lot of expenses so you can put a certain percentage into savings for every dollar you make. Start at 10%, then 12% and keep going until you are comfortable with living on a certain of what you earn. This takes discipline. If you work, get what you like, but make sure it doesn't cause you to spend everything you earn. It may take a couple weeks, a few months, or even years to save up for what you want but it'll be worth it.

Investing is when you take your money, put it into something and that something gives you ROI (Return-on-Investment). It's when your money is working for you even while you sleep sometimes. It could be immediate gains, or it could take years for the return on your investment to show. Again, just as a steady savings habit will help you in the long run, investing on a steady basis will be very beneficial if done properly.

Always help when you can. Put a little money to the side to help as well. It makes you feel good to be able to help someone in need.

CALL TO ACTION:

This week, look at online savings accounts, start researching ways to invest and grow your money at your age. Look for a charity or non-profit organization you may be able to help either through giving a little of your resources or your time.

Start now, you'll be glad you did.

NOTES

MONEY MOVES

By: Miguel Bravo

Market Manager

A couple of months ago, one of my good work buddies asked me to help him out with a project he was working on, and I agreed to, but like always, I waited until the last minute. I was stressed because the deadline was the next day. I didn't procrastinate on the project because I didn't value his friendship. I procrastinated the project because I didn't pay attention in school when they wanted to teach me how to write a paragraph on the typewriter. The same project that takes someone an hour to complete probably takes me a half day. I have a decent paying Store Manager job that requires little typing, but a lot of social skills. Had I had someone to guide me in the right direction when I was a young man, I would have gladly taken the advice and I may have been in a better situation than I am now. Please don't get me wrong, I love my job and I love my current life, but I wish I had made some better choices when I was young. Therefore, I am here today to help guide you in the next chapter that we call LIFE.

A little backstory on me, I am a 43-year-old man who was born and raised in a farm community in Southern California. My parents both came from Mexico to the U.S. when they were young. They both found work picking strawberries at a local farm in Oxnard, California. Spanish was my first language and my parents never really learned English. It was cool back in the day because I could tell my parents that I was done with my homework because they couldn't understand the curriculum anyway. I would go to bed without completing my homework. I was that kid who delivered the newspaper every day, the kid who mowed everyone's lawn, and the kid who survived in school not by having good grades but by having perfect attendance.

In high school, I had all advanced placement classes because I was intelligent. However, I switched to regular classes because that's where my friends were. I hung out with the popular kids; the kids who smoked weed before class, the kids who ditched class for parties, and the kids who liked the "street" life. After I graduated high school, I got a decent paying job at Home Depot. Some of my friends went to work with their parents, some picked up a trade, some went to college, and the others went to jail.

During my tenure at Home Depot, I used my strong work ethic and busted my butt every day without ever calling in sick and moved my way up the retail corporate ladder. After 7 years in the company, a couple of promotions, and a salary increase of 150%, I decided to take my talents elsewhere. I landed a job as a store manager at the age of 23 years old. I didn't know how to run a store at first, but I asked a lot of questions and worked 60 hours a week because I wanted to be the best store manager that I could be. Three years later, I was asked to relocate to San Diego, California where we were going to open a new store. My boss thought it would be a perfect fit for me because I was bilingual. I didn't want to leave my hometown because I loved my family, and I loved my homies but decided that the move would be best. Today, I have a wife, 2 kids, a parrot, and a dog. I still have the same job that I got when I was 23. I don't really drink (maybe a 6 pack a month) and I never got into drugs, and I absolutely love my life!

Even though I love my life, I wish I had done things differently. Remember those friends I told you that went to jail? Some of those guys are gone now. They either overdosed on cocaine or are working a hard job at minimum wage. My friends that are doing well in life are the ones who either learned a trade or went to college. They all have good paying jobs, nice cars, nice homes, and a lot of money. I don't regret working at the same job for the past 20 years, but I regret not going to college and working at the same time. Had I gone to college, I would have learned how to read and write better, I would have learned more about business finances, and I would have learned how to communicate better with people. This has helped me land a corporate job with the same company but with three times more money than I am currently making. My friends with college degrees have less people telling them what to do. They go on more vacations, and they have more freedom to do whatever they want, especially on weekends.

My two greatest regrets are not saving any money and not investing my money when I was young. The $10.00 that I spent on beer every month could have been invested in Amazon stock and I would have been a millionaire by now. Had I invested into my company's 401k fund for the past 20 plus years, I would have had enough money to retire by now, but I didn't. The good news for me is that, rather than saying "It's too late for me to start", I made myself learn about the stock market and 401k. I invested in several companies, bought some bitcoin, and maxed out my 401k. Pretty good for a homie in the hood! I am here today begging you to pay attention in school, go to college or learn a trade, and invest your money because money isn't everything, but life is a lot easier with it.

CALL TO ACTION:

Step 1: What do you want to do when you get older?

- If it's being a cop, ask a cop for a ride along.

- If it's being a Store Manager somewhere. Ask the Store Manager if you can spend some time with them at work.

- If you want to learn a trade, ask that person what steps they had to take to land that job.

Remember to ask about pension plans, 401k, and benefits.

Step 2: Where do you want to continue your education?

- Is at a trade school.

- Is it the military?

- Is it a College or University?

Remember to ask how much more money a person with a college degree makes compared to someone without a college degree.

Step 3: Investments:

- Find out what a credit score and credit report are and how they can help you.

- Find out what a 401k plan is.

- Pick 3 places where you would invest your money in the stock market. If I were to give you $100 to invest wherever you wanted and let you keep the earnings, some of you would become millionaires and some of you would still have $100 after 20 years. Don't be the guy with $100. Do your homework and be a millionaire!

NOTES

MONEY– THE ROOT OF ALL EVIL OR THE KEY TO THE GOOD LIFE?

By: Jeremy Black

Real Estate Technology/ Entrepreneur

In order to get things done in this life, you are going to need money. Cash or credit, either option, when married with the correct knowledge, will give you access to the best things this world has to offer. But why do our people not have it; or if they do have it, why do they not have the knowledge to know how to use it?

There are a few answers to the question, but instead of focusing on the why, let's now turn our attention on how to gain the knowledge of how to use it. Because once you learn how to find and use money, the opportunities that have been right in front of your eyes will now become clear.

Let me first start with a personal anecdote. In 2012, I was an18-year-old freshman in college. A few weeks before arriving on campus, I went to Wells Fargo to open a bank account. About an hour later, had a checking and savings account. Before completing the final pages of required paperwork, the banker asked me if I would like to apply for a CREDIT CARD. Excited, but having a vague understanding of how credit works, I eagerly said yes, and before I knew it, I had a red piece of plastic with a five-hundred-dollar limit! The advice I received from my mother at the time regarding the card was., "Make your payments on time for six months, and then pay the card off in full to have the best credit score." This advice was not too terrible, but since then, I have discovered the best ways to get and keep a high credit score.

Credit is important, because unless you have mountains of cash lying around for every purchase that you want to make, credit is how you will buy your house, car, rent an apartment, and even obtain some jobs. Credit, in its simplest definition, is how a bank feels about your ability to pay back a loan given to you. For example, if you are wanting to buy a car, a person with a low credit score will be less likely to get a loan from a bank to buy the car; or if they are approved, the bank will charge a higher interest rate (An interest rate = the cost of borrowing money. If I lend you 100 dollars and charge you 10% interest, you will pay me a total of $110), because that person is seen as a risk to lend money too. So, if you are thinking about obtaining your first credit card, please consider if you can pay it back. f you don't, you may not be able to obtain a house, car or job in the future.

Some quick tips for those who have their first card or now have bad credit:

1. Remember that no matter how bad your credit score is, it can always be repaired and restored.

2. Never use more than 30% percent of your credit limit. So, if your limit is $1,500, never use more than $450 a month. Using more than this amount will significantly hurt your credit score.

3. If you have parents, friends, loved ones that have great credit scores, ask their permission to become an authorized user of their card. Now it is important to note that you do not have to be physically using or swiping their card. If the cardholder has excellent history of paying their bills on time, keeping their usage low, and having high credit limits- this will help you tremendously, as this may be the best way for you to build your credit before you are able to legally obtain one!

Investing basically means having your money work for you. There are multiple ways of doing this, but for the sake of keeping this chapter short, I will discuss investing in stocks. Not too long ago, when I was in high school, all the cool kids wore Jordans. Whether it was for style or sport, you were considered a part of the "in-crowd" if you owned at least one pair. I was not able to afford my first pair until years later, but this is when I realized that owning a share of the company that makes Jordans (Nie) costs less than the actual shoe. At the time of this writing, the price of Nike stock is $130. Considering the price of any retro Jordan shoe bought at retail is at least $170, you can own a piece of the company for less than what the shoe costs. Anyone 18 years old or older (those younger will need the permission of their parent or guardian) with access to a smart phone, download the Robinhood or TD Ameritrade app and start buying the companies you spend all your money on. Own an iPhone, AirPods, iPad, and a MacBook? Buy shares in the company that makes those products! Apple! Love using social media apps such as Facebook and Instagram? Well, I have good news for you! Buying into Facebook gives ownership of both platforms!

Investing does not have to be hard or scary. There are plenty of resources for you to learn from. Securing your financial future starts with you taking the initial steps to educate yourselves in areas that have not been taught to us. Remember that you can shape your future as well as the future of generations to come.

NOTES

IN THE VALLEY

By: Damar Christopher

Sr. Director, Product Management

"Even though I walk through the darkest valley, I will fear no evil . . ." Psalms 23:4 NIV

According to the Oxford Languages Dictionary, "a valley is a low area between hills or mountains typically with a river running through it. In geology, a valley or dale is a depression that is longer than it is wide."

This definition is significant because it gives the impression that it is impossible or unlikely that a person in the valley can simply climb their way out; there are steep mountains or hills on their left and right. It is also remarkable that most valleys typically have water flowing through them. The assumption is that over time the water has eroded the land to form the valley and is now limited by the land formation it created.

In life it is inevitable we will have a "valley" experience. Parents divorce, loved ones die, relationships end, or jobs are lost. These valleys happen and we suddenly find ourselves in a dark place with seemingly no way out. However, the truth is, there are always lessons to learn in the valley so that you emerge better than when you went in.

Lesson 1: Submit to the Process

As men, one of the most difficult things we can do is submit. Many times, our pride and ego get in the way of our learning. However, there is usually deep and meaningful growth that can occur while we are having a valley experience.

If relationships end painfully, you can examine your role in the pain. Did you contribute to the issues that caused the relationship to end? Are there flaws in your character or thinking that are unhealthy and need to change? Are these changes you can make yourself, or do you need an honest and open conversation with loved ones or professionals to help you understand and own your issues?

If a loved one passes away, do you believe you should have done something different? Spent more time with them or expressed your love more? If so, take the time to look at your other relationships and make them better while you have the time.

The point is that you don't ignore or bury the pain, but you embrace it, learn from it, and emerge better as a result.

Lesson 2: Find the Root Cause

Sometimes we find ourselves in a valley through no fault of our own. But, if we're being honest, sometimes we create our own valleys through poor choices and destructive patterns of behavior.

Being in a valley gives you the opportunity to meditate on your own behavior and consider how the outcome could have been different if the actions you took were different. Could you have offered a compliment instead of an insult? Could you have chosen to forgive rather than hold a grudge? Could you help make situations better rather than listing everything that is wrong? Could you have studied or worked harder, rather than procrastinating or playing video games?

The river that runs through our personal valleys is often our own actions that have robbed us of what we truly want and now we find ourselves suffering from the natural consequences of those actions.

There is always hope though: identify the destructive pattern of behavior and change it.

CALL TO ACTION:

Please take some time this week to do some reflection and complete this simple exercise:

1. Write down the 1-2 things that cause you the most pain (your valleys).

2. Write down why those things hurt you so much.

3. Write down how you may have contributed to your own pain (your rivers).

4. Decide what you will do differently going forward to learn from the pain and grow into a better person.

NOTES

THE ANTIDOTE FOR FEAR

By: Bryan Henriquez

Entrepreneur

The antidote for fear is ACTION! They say there's a lot of dreams, discoveries, and riches at a graveyard! Individuals who were meant for greatness but never reached their purpose because of the fear that paralyzed them. When I heard this, I made a promise to myself that no matter what my circumstances are, I never want to live with regret or say the statements "I should have or what if." On August 08, 2015, at a Sonic in Grand Prairie, Texas, my business partner Caio and I began to brainstorm different services we can provide to the people of Texas! We targeted the construction field, from renting dumpsters to masonry work. We had hundreds of ideas on a napkin. By the end of the night Caio blurred out "how about concrete pumping". He was already in the field. Our other two partners had been doing this for years, so why not? We did our research and began to save up. I worked two jobs and had a side cleaning hustle. At the same time, my wife and I were planning and saving up for our wedding.

In less than a year, I got married and Warrior concrete pumping was launched. Three months into my marriage, I was working two jobs and part time at the concrete business. I was getting overwhelmed, but I knew that I had to persevere! Sitting at my desk, I said "Bryan if you want to see Warrior grow and be a key player in the Construction field, you need to give it 110% and more. It was at that moment I knew that I had to leave both of my jobs. God will bring people to push and bring the greatness out of you. He knew my wife would be that person! When bringing this to her she said, "Bryan it's a scary move, but I challenge you in this. Quit your jobs and let's give it a month. If you can bring a month's salary by going all in, then we will move forward. If not, you will need to get a job." Challenge accepted!

That entire month I was laughed at, cursed out, and heard the word "NO" over 100 times. On some days, I had meetings, and I was stood up! Fear will begin to creep in. The fear of failure, fear of acceptance, and the fear of financial woes. After the third week, I said "enough and I have to switch it up." I started to create different systems and strategies. I pushed my fears away. I started to hate and get angry at all the lies and fears. So much that I wanted to destroy who I was and the purpose of Warrior concrete.

August 25,2020, four years later, the company has grown in units and in clients. The best career decision I ever made. Did it get easy after that first month? Hell no! But every day you take action to overcome fear. Fear will destroy your purpose, your relationships and everything around you. Action is what we need, to move fear out of the way. Your fears are not greater than your purpose. Change and success will come when you face and begin to hate your fears. Hate your fears with a passion because if not it will take your passion away! We were born to act not to sit. When we allow fear to overcome us, we become immobile. When you become immobile your dreams and purpose begin to die. When they die all, you have is the ashes of, "I should have or what if", laid out at the cemetery.

John Maxwell says, "A leader is one who knows the way, goes the way and shows the way". My challenge to everyone who reads this is, be more than just words and dreams, challenge yourself to take action!

CALL TO ACTION:

The key things to help overcome fear:

- Identify your fears.

- Face your fears

- Create a plan to overcome it.

- Execute a plan.

- Surround yourself with a good community. The biggest misconception we have especially for men is that we believe we can do it alone.

- Above all things **PRAY**!

NOTES

GRIT

By: Dante Seay

Engineer, Entrepreneur

Having the ambitions to create a goal leads to a cycle that people struggle with regularly. Set the goal, try, fail, rinse, and repeat until it is done, or not. Some people have a problem with following through and finishing what they start. There is a major trait that separates the person who settles from the finisher. Grit. This means to pursue a goal regardless of the distractions or hurdles that can and will come up. Having some grit can potentially change your life for the better, or in my case, help finish college with an engineering degree. I started college with the, "I will settle with a different major if it gets difficult" mindset, but that changed when I zeroed in on a few personal areas.

First and foremost, who are you accomplishing this task for. I've learned that a person will work at a completely different level when they are doing something for someone they love. Oftentimes, when a person is trying to complete a goal for themselves, they formulate excuse on top of excuse as to why they can't finish the task. Some people don't have the discipline necessary to hold themselves accountable if they fail at the goal they set. Making the goal for someone other than yourself will not only give you a stronger drive, but it will also add passion to the task at hand. I know personally, if I am working with my wife on my mind, laziness will disappear into thin air and my focus goes through the roof!

The second topic to zero in on is to make sure the goal or task interests you. It is much easier to pursue something that you don't dread doing. It is well known that many people do not enjoy waking up early to go work a job that doesn't interest them. When there is interest in the task, you can't wait to wake up and get back on the grind. Oftentimes, knowing the end goal of the task helps add excitement to the work. Understanding that getting a college degree has the potential to create wealth and maintain your livelihood was enough to add excitement to my studies. With interest comes curiosity, and with curiosity comes the drive to dive deeper!

Lastly, you must practice. In the college scenario, this means getting those study hours every day. The more you practice, the easier the task will become. This becomes more than the well-known saying, practice makes perfect. When you're practicing, you are taking the time to get to know the subject at hand. When you practice enough, it becomes more than just practice. It becomes an art form. This is equivalent to performing at an elite level and when you are this comfortable with the task, it doesn't seem like a chore, you are now perfecting your art!

Several people find themselves in that rinse and repeat cycle in year one of going to college. Focusing on my who, making sure my goal was interesting to myself, and practicing daily helped give me the grit I needed to finish college. My example can be substituted for any type of goal or task that people are faced with in their everyday life. There will always be challenges that you must face but listening to wisdom and acting accordingly will separate you from the bunch. Dr. Eric Thomas said it best, "When you want to succeed as bad as you want to breathe, then you'll be successful!". Grit is perseverance. Do you, have it?

CALL TO ACTION:

I challenge you to take five minutes and write out your three personal areas to focus on that were discussed in the paragraphs above. Afterwards, get back on the grind while focusing on those three areas!

NOTES

4TH QUARTER

REACHING YOUR GOALS

A WEEK OF PRAISE

By: Dr. Kevin D. Williams

Minister

This is a week of praise. David the psalmist says:

Psalms 150:6 Let everything that hath breath praise the Lord. Praise ye the Lord. KJV

Today many young men are faced with challenges and may have the question, where is my place? In this present society of "Black Lives Matter", is there any room for me at the table? Our President campaigned on we must take America back and let us make America great again. Take it back from who? His predecessor looked like me, did he steal it? Why is it that men and young men of color are constantly killed? Am I on the endangered species list? All of these are great questions that merit answers from those who can provide them. **Where is the praise or my praise in the midst of it all?**

In looking for answers to our questions and direction for daily living, I believe it would be most helpful to turn to the word of

God. Solomon, the writer of Proverbs, has something remarkably interesting to say.

Proverbs 1:7-10

7 Fear of the Lord is the foundation of true knowledge, but fools despise wisdom and discipline.

A Father's Exhortation: Acquire Wisdom

8 My child, listen when your father corrects you. Don't neglect your mother's instruction.

9 What you learn from them will crown you with grace and be a chain of honor around your neck.

10 My child, if sinners entice you, turn your back on them!

Holy Bible, New Living Translation

Our praise and our success will develop with faith and obedience to God. Surrendering to the Will of God and having the wisdom to know His expectations.

FAITH and OBEDIENCE

This is a great message to help free the minds of our young men. As Solomon was guided by the Holy Spirit, it allowed him to be able to provide advice that would be applicable to today. At the root of the problems we have, Satan (the devil). Online digital pornography, legalization of marijuana, same sex marriages, under education and unemployment are problems that face the neighborhoods of perhaps most of our reading audience. Solomon instructs his readers to know *"The fear of the Lord is the foundation of true knowledge."* For you to have an opportunity to make it, one must start with the solid foundation of fearing God. Fearing God in essence, is reverential respect for God. Even if you are not familiar with what is written in the bible, just having enough respect to fear God must be the foundation upon which all other stones are laid. After all God has given us all things that pertain to life and godliness. Fearing God is not experiencing tremors at the very thought of God, like many are now having when in the presence of the police.

Fear of God is basically respect for who He is. When facing death, literally being burned alive in the fiery furnace of king Nebuchadnezzar. There were three Hebrew boys; Shadrach, Meshach and Abednego who had so much integrity and respect for God they would not compromise their principals. The king wanted them and all others to bow down and worship a golden image he created. They could have easily complied with his decree; however, they withstood king Nebuchadnezzar by telling him "If it be so, our God who is able shall deliver us out of this furnace and out of your hands. *But if not, let it be known we will not serve thy gods or worship the golden image that you have set up." (Daniel 3:15-18).* These young men in their youth had decided obedience to God is better than worldly acceptance. The benefits were noticeably clear, the men who had the task of casting Shadrach, Meshach and Abednego into the exceptionally hot furnace were burned. At the same time not a hair on their heads was singed nor did they smell like what they had come out of. God was with them in the fire, the same as His son Jesus Christ is with us today.

Unfortunately, today most do not know or are aware of the need to fear the Lord. From the White House to the house where you and I live, the respect for God at a high level does not exist. Parents have an awesome responsibility to instill into the next generation the word of God. The apostle Paul had some positive words for the Corinthians.

2 Corinthians 7:1

Having therefore these promises, dearly beloved, let us cleanse ourselves from all filthiness of the flesh and spirit, perfecting holiness in the fear of God. KJV

SURRENDER

To cleanse ourselves from all filthiness of the flesh means we must deny ourselves some things. Jesus has said in Luke 9:23. If I can be real for a moment, it is a lot easier for me to tell you no before I say no to myself. All of us are in this same predicament, it just depends on what we really need to say no to. Sometimes we cannot go to certain places, be around a group because of the temptation that awaits us. If we struggle with certain issues, it is best not to have yourself in the environment knowing it is too much to handle.

Paul challenges the Corinthians to glorify God with their bodies (I Corinthians 6:19-20). He tells the church at Ephesus to control what you say.

Ephesians 4:29

Let no corrupt communication proceed out of your mouth, but that which is good to the use of edifying, that it may minister grace unto the hearers. KJV

Our speech cannot mimic the salty language we hear in most stand-up comedy. As a child of God or God's children it is not expected for one to walk around saying praise the Lord all day, but we cannot sound and act like the world either. We have been set to a higher standard and expectations.

Solomon encourages us to "listen".

Proverbs 1:8

My child, listen when your father corrects you. Don't neglect your mother's instruction Holy Bible, New Living Translation

Solomon is teaching the need to be responsible with information you receive. In other words, use the knowledge you have learned. Being accountable to God's Word is an awesome responsibility. When one is familiar with the word of God, he or she can skillfully use it to draw others out of the world or at the least have an alert conscience of behavior. Self-control will not only help you, but it will also help others as well. It will cause others to wonder and inquire as to how you have so much composure when the wheels are falling off the wagon. How can you not indulge when it is so tempting? People not only pay attention to what you say, they notice your behavior.

This compliments the instruction the Apostle Paul provided to the young Evangelist Timothy

I Timothy 4:13

Till I come, give attendance to reading, to exhortation, to doctrine. KJV

WISDOM

He instructs Timothy to become a student of the word of God. When one becomes a student of learning he/she will see a positive outcome in life. It is not an instant process; it is ongoing work and commitment and a desire to obtain and retain information. Being a student is giving daily attention to transforming ourselves by the renewing of our minds into the image of God (Romans 12:1-2).

Again, Solomon writes:

Proverbs 1:10

My child, if sinners entice you, turn your back on them!

Holy Bible, New Living Translation

Proverbs 1:15

My child don't go along with them! Stay far away from their paths.

Holy Bible, New Living Translation

CALL TO ACTION:

To rise above, you must separate from that which holds you down. In the 2004 movie Ray, a biopic of the life of recording artist Ray Charles. Actor Jamie Foxx portrayed Ray Charles, there was scene in the movie at a roadside restroom where members of the band were doing drugs. Ray wanted to have the experience of being high to forget or numb the pain of his past. Fathead his trumpet player tried to discourage Ray from participating and even told him: *"it's your own funeral"*. The same is true today, when one decides to blatantly go against the word of God, it is your own funeral. We have the responsibility and power of choices and decisions for our lives. Use this gift wisely and never take it for granted.

Paul again instructs Timothy to:

II Timothy 2:22

Flee also youthful lusts: but follow righteousness, faith, charity, peace, with them that call on the Lord out of a pure heart. KJV

I believe we can have a week of praise, knowing each day we may not have been perfect but striving to be found faithful. Let us experience an abundant life in Jesus Christ.

John 10:10

The thief cometh not, but for to steal, and to kill, and to destroy. I am come that they might have life, and that they might have it more abundantly.   *KJV*

NOTES

MAKE THE MOST OF EACH DAY

By: Mark Kim

Finance

Your mind possesses immense power, and it's crucial to cultivate a positive mental attitude, regardless of your present circumstances. Maximize the potential of the one life you've been given, here's how-

Thoughts to start your day:

- Think of 5 things you are grateful for. Work at having a glass half-full mentality. You can only choose your actions and attitude. People want to be around people with good attitudes. If you cannot think of anything, here are some examples. There are no right or wrong answers here.

  o Health, food, something someone did for you, etc.

- What 3 things do you want to accomplish today?

- o This does not have to be big things but what gets you to set priorities and feel like you have accomplished something amid all the chaos of the day.

- o Celebrate this as a victory at the end of the day.

- Make your bed – it is a simple task that you can complete right after you get up to set your mind on completing things.

Thoughts for the day:

- Be responsible with your money – you work hard for it.

  - o Work on saving 15% of what you make. Live within your means and do not spend more than you make. Staying out of debt is very freeing and allows you to be in a position of strength if things go bad.

  - o Can you save $7 a day? This does not seem like much, but that is $210 a month and over $2,500 a year.

- Be willing and ready to help others. They will appreciate it and you will feel better about yourself. They could potentially return the favor in the future, although do not expect it.

- Surround yourself with good, caring, positive people. Always work on giving more than you receive, but do not be shy in asking for help. Distance yourself from the "takers" (who always want something but are not willing to give back) and the negative people. The mind is powerful - fill it with positive energy. Good things happen to good people.

- Work on learning something new each day. This will help you grow as a person and send you down paths you never thought possible. Education and knowledge lift people to new places.

- Reach out and meet someone new. Understanding people and their perspectives will help you go farther in life. Be open to new ways and ideas.

CALL TO ACTION:

Thoughts for the end of the day:

At the end of the day, for the things that you did, would you be proud to put your name next to them? If they showed up as a story on the front page of the paper, would your mother or Grandmother be proud to see it? If you were the boss, would you have paid yourself for the work you did?

- o Work on doing things well, keeping your word, and being a finisher. Too many people like starting things. Successful people finish things.

- o It takes years to build a reputation and only minutes to ruin it.

NOTES

UNAPOLOGETICALLY YOU

By: Devin Christopher

Co-Working/Community Manager

As you're growing up there are a few questions and statements you'll grow familiar with as you slowly begin to understand who you are, what talents you possess and what you like to do. Questions like "how can you make money from this?" and "wow you're talented." One of the biggest questions throughout my life has always been "what are you going to do?" and it always puzzled me. Such a broad question exceeded my understanding mainly because it involved growing up. And growing up involved doing things I didn't want to do so the answer was simple for me. The same thing I've been doing; whatever I wanted without the responsibility or consequence of my actions.

I soon found out that this wasn't a realistic option and I had to reevaluate myself and talents and ask the people around me what I was good at, or what they could see me doing. Another reason why that question always stumped me was because it sounded so final. At one point in my life, I wanted that minimum wage job. The next day I changed my mind and that's ok - life affords us the luxury of making a choice at any given time and changing our trajectory completely. The biggest thing is just being willing to take a step, no matter how small in the right direction. Today I can confidently say I don't know if what I'm doing is exactly what I was made for, but what I do know is that I'm on the right track and that confidence spreads to every area of my life making the daily decisions a lot easier.

In the world today with the influence of social media it is impossible to live without comparing yourself to your contemporaries, your idols and even the people who are younger than you. Whether it's age, money, possessions, etc., there will always be someone better than you in some regard. The good news is *it's not a competition.* Contrary to popular belief, the only person you are competing with day in, and day out is yourself! Every day you make a conscious decision to do or be more, no matter how small, is another day you've won. In my opinion the best thing you can do is document your growth, struggles, dreams, everything. For some people the best way to see their own evolution is writing it down, while for others it may be something else entirely. The way I like to track my growth is by talking with other people who have known me for an extended amount of time and can see the changes a lot easier than I can and in turn we can be accountability partners for each other.

CALL TO ACTION:

My challenge is to ask the people in your life who have a voice - how would they describe you? What are your strengths/weaknesses? Does that motivate you or bother you? Most importantly, what are you going to do about it? All it takes is a little time and attention. In a month, six months, a year or even 10 years, you can be in a completely different place looking back on the person you were with gratitude. You just must take it one step at a time.

NOTES

HANDLING DISAPPOINTMENT

By: Otis Idlebird

Entrepreneur

In order to understand how to handle disappointment, let us get a good definition for disappointment.

dis·ap·point·ment: sadness or displeasure caused by the nonfulfillment of one's hopes or expectations.

In your life you will have hopes or expectations and as sure as you have hopes and expectations for your life, you will have disappointments. Disappointments, if we do not understand what they are and how to deal with them, can cause you to be burdened with the stress of sadness and displeasure for not meeting the expectations.

ex·pec·ta·tion: a strong belief that something will happen or be the case in the future.

The hopes and expectations are the goals which you want to achieve. With anything that you set out to do, there are some perceived and some actual thoughts as to how these expectations can be met. You perceived that building a go cart is easy to do.

When you begin to build your go cart, you realize that it is pretty hard for you. The expectation becomes the motivator and the action plan until the actual building of the go cart takes place. Sawing, nailing, painting, brakes, wheels, money, rope, seat, measuring tape and a place to build, are all actual steps that are needed that may exceed your initial expectations. You ask your parents or guardian for the money and the place to build your go cart and they say, not right now, maybe later. Disappointment in this situation is hearing your parents or guardian say no. Disappointment can also come from being able to start the building of the go cart and stopping when the actual effort becomes too difficult. Every day that you walk past that go cart is a reminder of that unfulfilled expectation.

Your expectations can be as simple as receiving a desired gift. If that expectation is the latest most popular game console, then your expectation is to get the best. How would you feel if you were given the Atari system, a popular game console in the 80's? Will you feel sadness or displeasure for the non-fulfillment of your expectation? I believe we are getting on the same page when it comes to disappointment.

Expectations touch our lives in many ways: education, employment, opportunities, long term goals, short term goals, possessions, and status in society. How we go about achieving those expectations will begin to shape in your mind, whether the expectation is too high, low, achievable, or unrealistic. Unrealistic expectations assume a level of control that we don't have in a situation. We repeatedly feel disappointment that the expectation hasn't been met.

There are some expectations that rely very heavily on you to complete and shoulder the results. You will have outcomes of some expectations which are beyond your ability to complete without the efforts of others.

Life should be fair but it's not. Disappointment comes when you continue to expect fairness and continue to come up short. Don't be disappointed when someone does not like you even when you are nice to them. Believing that you will fail will no doubt come true and will disappoint you despite the failing expectation. God's word gives us a story of expectations, disappointments, and achievements in the person of Naaman.

Read 2 Kings 5:1-15 (KJV)

We see that Naaman, a captain in Syria had leprosy. It was understood that the prophet of God in Samaria could heal him of his leprosy. With permission from the King of Syria, Naaman carried a letter and servants to the King of Israel. The King of Israel considers this act to be an act of aggression. Elisha hears and asks that Naaman, and his servants come to him. Naaman and his company came and stood at the door of Elisha. In verse 10, Elisha's servant came to the door and told Naaman to go and wash in the Jordan 7 times, his flesh will be restored, and he will be clean. Naaman became angry! Why did Naaman become angry?

Naaman had an expectation of how he wanted to be healed. He even outlined his inner thoughts verbally. Verse 11 says, he thought that Elisha would have come out to him and stand and call on the name of the Lord and wave his hand over the spot. He even listed better rivers in Damascus than the Jordan in Israel to dip in. EXPECTATIONS! When Naaman's expectations were not met he was angry, dissatisfied, sad and disappointed. Naaman's servant had to help him understand the reality of his expectations. It was not what the prophet told him to do. If he had told you to do any of those things, would you have done those things? Why not do what the prophet says? Naaman then goes and follows the prophet's instructions, and his flesh was restored to the skin of a young boy. Naaman's goal was to be cleansed. When he was cleansed, he was no longer disappointed. He was satisfied with the results.

Wikipedia says that "Disappointment is a subjective response related to anticipated rewards. " Disappointment can take a few minutes as in Naaman's case or for others the same disappointment can take a few days or even longer depending on the severity of the disappointment.

How do you recover from disappointing circumstances?

CALL TO ACTION:

1. Be honest with yourself about the situations that have you disappointed.

2. Be objective about the facts and the outcome of the unmet expectations.

3. Don't wallow in regret for too long. Get back in the game of living.

4. Make sure your expectations are realistic.

5. Forgive yourself!

6. Learn the lesson about you and how you handled the situation.

7. Find a different approach.

When you factor the Lord into any situation, He makes all things possible. Even when your expectations are not met, knowing that the Lord brings possibility makes up the difference when you can't seem to get close to your high expectations on your own. He also makes your disappointments easier to deal with.

May the Lord bless and keep you.

NOTES

HANDLING DISAPPOINTMENT

By: Trent Hamilton

FAA Construction Manager

FACT…..You will experience disappointment as long as you are living on this earth! It's a natural consequence in every human being's life, and it's something we all must deal with, like it or not. The feelings of disappointment can come from so many sources, and many of them will be minor. However, some will be very significant. You may experience disappointment with your parents, your siblings or other family members, your friends, teachers, co-workers, or church members. Disappointments may come from people in the public eye, such as athletes, entertainers, state & government officials, and even the President of the U.S. You may also face disappointments through private relationships, such as marriage, courtship, close friendships or spiritual relationships. Lastly, you will experience disappointment in yourself! The bottom line is, disappointment will continue to be present, and the question for you is, how are you going to handle it when it does?

From childhood I grew to be a huge Dallas Cowboy fan. I'm sure you're thinking "the Cowboys?" Yeah… I know. So, of course I know about disappointment! I'm talking about over 25 years from 1997 to 2021, and counting, of …continuous disappointment. My young adult children have asked me how I could continue to route for a team who has been on the losing end for over 2-1/2 decades. Well, when I first became a fan as a young kid in the 1970's, the Cowboys were one of the best teams in the NFL, which lasted through the 1990's. They won 5 Super Bowl Championships through that span, and life was good as a Cowboy fan! I explained to my children that even though I've endured so many years of disappointment, I still root for them and support them, because of the joy I once had when they were the best team in the league. I have faith that one day they will return to championship status.

So how does this story relate to my message for you? There will be many more meaningful levels of disappointment in your life. Sometimes you may experience disappointment from someone who has provided years of joy and happiness in the past, but this one time…. they failed to do so. When that happens, try to exercise forgiveness and understanding. Also strive to have that same level of hope and faith that I have for the Cowboys and remember that "it will get better one day!"

When it comes to handling disappointment, I recommend three steps to consider, which may help you overcome it. First, you must permanently in-bed in your mind that disappointments will happen, and you must try to prepare for it when it does. Secondly, once disappointment arrives, you must choose the proper response and decide on your next direction to take. Lastly, you must have a dependable source by which you receive encouragement and guidance on how to move forward.

God is the ultimate example on being prepared for disappointment. From the time we were born, He knew we would do something against his will. It started with Adam and Eve, then later with Moses and the Children of Israel, continuing with the discipleship of Jesus Christ, and now during this current day. Every time we disappoint God, he already knew and was prepared. Through his matchless grace and mercy, he allowed his son Jesus to cover our failures through his death. So, when you think about that, how will you prepare for disappointments? If it happens with someone close to you, like a family member or friend, what will be your next move? You may experience multiple emotions such as sadness, anger, humor, disbelief, or excitement. The first decision to make is a proper response. You must ask yourself, is this something you can handle or is it too much to bear? The path you select to address your emotions will have a positive or negative impact on how you move forward.

There is a right way and a wrong way to deal with disappointments. Which path will you choose? To correctly respond to disappointment, you should plan on the best path to take. When you depend on people, you must expect that disappointment is a possibility. Based on the relationship you have with that person: it may dictate your next approach with them. If you truly love someone, you should not allow disappointments to completely end the relationship. Just as God continues to love us despite our mistakes, we should work to have the same response for those we love and care for, regardless of their failures. In many instances, that person did not intend to disappoint you.

Often disappointments may occur because you did not get the job you really wanted, or you were not able to purchase the house or car you desired, or you couldn't preserve that relationship with your significant other. There are so many levels of disappointment, however you can still take the same approach for each of them. You must find a way to make that negative event into a positive one. It doesn't mean giving up and moving to something else. Sometime this is the best option. Instead, you may need to work a little harder to get what you desire. Just remember that how you respond to disappointment can have a lasting effect on your life. So, make sure you seek the right path.

Lastly, what I believe is the most important action to take when handling disappointment is having a dependable source to receive encouragement and guidance. There may be many forms of disappointment that you can handle on your own. However, there will also be other disappointments which may be so impactful to your life, that you may need help! As I stated before, there is no one on this earth who has not experienced disappointment. I advise you to find someone whom you can confide in, to help encourage and guide you through it.

The most obvious being that I recommend for help, is our Father God! He's the ultimate expert on dealing with disappointment and is clearly the best source for you to go to, no matter what level of disappointment you're dealing with. The avenue of prayer will help direct your path. In addition to our heavenly Father, you should also have one or more individuals to commune with, who will have your best interest in mind. In many instances, it is unwise to try to defeat disappointment on your own. Utilizing these valuable resources will help you overcome this problem.

One of my most favorite scriptures in the bible is Proverbs 3:5-6, which states, **"Trust in the Lord with all your heart and lean not on your own understanding. In all your ways submit to him, and he will make your path straight."**

Another scripture I love is found in the book of Isaiah 40:31, which states, **"But those who wait on the Lord shall renew their strength: they shall mount up with wings like eagles, they shall run and not be weary, and they shall walk and not faint.**

CALL TO ACTION:

As I conclude, it's my hope that if you don't get anything else out of what I have written on this topic of "handling disappointment", please allow those scriptures that you just read to resonate in your mind. If you believe in God's word, that is a great start to getting past disappointment. The three steps I discussed of, 1) understanding and preparing, 2) choosing the proper response and direction, and 3) having a dependable source for guidance and direction, can surely help you with handling disappointment.

May God bless you with this certain challenge in life! TVH

NOTES

WEEK 46:

HANDLING DISAPPOINTMENT(II CORINTHIANS 12:7-10)

By: Autavius Hobbs

Pharmacy Account Managers

Objective – To understanding that our disappointments are often opportunities for us to see that God is with us and that He is the source of our strength.

According to Websters dictionary, **disappointments** can be described as unhappiness from the failure of something hoped for or expected to happen. It can also be described as someone or something that fails to satisfy hopes and expectations. Some would describe disappointment as an emotion that typically brings forth sadness or sorrow. Disappointments are interesting in many ways, but what really stands out to me is its reputation for being "unbiased". It does not discriminate against age, gender, nationality, social class, economic class, Christianity, etc. Infants even experience disappointments if they are not fed or changed in a timely manner. If you have been living long enough, you have probably experienced disappointments. Our lesson today is designed to help us learn how we can better handle the disappointments that life will send our way.

Read II Corinthians 12:7-10 (ESV). These verses help us to see those disappointments if handled correctly, will help us see that God is with us and that He is the source of our strength. For the next few minutes, we will review some things about disappointments that help us prevent the sadness and sorrows that often weigh us down in life.

Disappointments have a way of **keeping us humble.** In a perfect world, we would all love for everything to work out in our favor. Many children dream and aspire to be wealthy, to go to the best university, and to become doctors, lawyers, musicians, professional athletes, etc. However, the reality is that things may not always go our way nor work out according to our plans. The Apostle Paul was able to see some things that others were not able to see. He was able to do some things that others were not able to do. His privileges could have easily led him to become conceited and feel like he was better than everyone else. Therefore, God allowed him to have a thorn in the flesh. We do not know for sure what his thorn in the flesh represented. However, we can confirm that this was unpleasant to him. This could be looked at as a disappointment for Paul, but we can also see that the purpose of the disappointment was to make sure that Paul did not allow his success or his visions to cause him to become arrogant or conceited. Disappointments have a way of keeping us **humble.**

Disappointments will also cause us to **call upon God for help.** When everything is going our way and everything that we do is successful, we tend to forget the source of our blessings. Our success often leads to self-admiration, and we begin to feel like we can do anything. Paul understood that his disappointments were beyond his control. Therefore, he called out to the Lord three times to ask if his thorn could be removed. The Bible helps us to see that this was not just a casual request but a plead, which emphasizes the desperation for God's help. We should all strive to be our best and always give our best. However, we must understand that our best will never supersede disappointments because God understands that these are the times that we will call on Him to help us.

Finally, disappointments can become **opportunities**. Paul quickly realized that some of his disappointments in life happened on purpose. At times they were inconvenient, frustrating, and humiliating. However, he began to understand that his disappointments were opportunities for God to give him strength. God was teaching him a lesson about hitting the reset button in life. Sometimes we drift away from God by leaning on our own strength, but God is more effective in our lives when we are weak because this gives Him the opportunity to build us up with His strength. When Paul figured this out his whole attitude about life changed. He went from complaining about disappointments to embracing them as opportunities.

CALL TO ACTION:

Make a list of any of the current worries and concerns that may have been recently weighing you down and causing you to feel disappointed.

Find a quiet place and send up a prayer to God asking Him to give you the strength to handle these disappointments in a way that brings Glory to His name. Also, ask God to give you strength to not stress over the things that you cannot control.

Read **Psalms 40** each day to remind yourself that God is your Help and your Deliverer.

Life is full of disappointments. Sometimes our disappointments derive from our own failed personal expectations and other times disappointments occur when people let us down. The response to these disappointments is emotions that often cause sadness and sorrow. Our goal is to handle our disappointments in a way that pleases God. When we remember that God is our help and our deliverer, we begin to understand that our disappointments are just opportunities for God to strengthen us, humble us and open our eyes to a joy and a peace that many people fail to understand.

 Lord, bless us with the wisdom to handle our disappointments in a way that puts a smile on your face.

NOTES

WORDS OF SUPPORT AND ENCOURAGEMENT TO MY YOUNG BROTHERS

By: Larry Chappell

Sales Leader President's Club

Text Reference: Esther Chapters 1 & 2 *(Please read)*

Even though there are many points and highlights in this text, I will not be long. I want to encourage you as you read this to always know GOD is with you. Not only is GOD with you, but he also goes before you. Not only does he go before you, but he also puts solutions and remedies in motion long before you know an issue, challenge, or situation exists.

Reading chapters 1 and 2 of Esther we can see GOD moving pieces to save HIS people before HIS people realize there's an issue and sets up their salvation. Whenever you find yourself facing issues, challenges, and situations in your life, you must know GOD had a solution before your issue became an issue.

Always know and be assured of the fact GOD is aware before you become aware.

In chapter 1 we see Vashti, the king's wife, being relieved of her position due to her behavior. GOD is creating a need for Vashti's replacement and an opportunity to put HIS child in a position to ultimately save HIS people. Does Esther or Mordecai know what's going on at this point? No. Are Esther and Mordecai aware a problem will emerge sometime in the very near future? No. But who knows? GOD! Because he remedies a problem before it exists.

In chapter 2 Esther is chosen by the king as his wife and in verse 17 the Bible says the king loved her. Also, in chapter 2 Mordecai foils a plot created by two men to kill the king (vs 21-23). Both of those events were opportunities for GOD to intervene and prepare a plan for HIS people to save HIS people with the participants before they were aware what was upon them. What a mighty, powerful, and loving GOD we serve to fix a problem before HIS people know one exists.

CALL TO ACTION:

Please read the whole book of Esther and focus on chapters 1 and 2. You will see how GOD has you and sets a plan in motion to deliver you before you are aware of your issue. We serve the same GOD that moved before Esther and Mordecai. We must know he is moving and going before us as well. Amen.

Stay encouraged, stay with GOD, and continue to live a life that one day you will hear, "Well done thy good and faithful servant."

In HIM, your brother,

Larry Chappell

NOTES

BE CONSISTENT

By: Trent Hamilton

FAA Construction Manager

The word "consistent" is defined as "constantly adhering (sticking to) principles or staying on course." It also means "holding firmly or fixed together." When you read those definitions, you may say to yourself, "that sounds pretty easy to do!" Or you may think, "I won't have any problems with being consistent." However, the reality is, as we continue to grow and live in this crazy world, staying consistent is a very difficult challenge.

I've been blessed with the privilege of having a relationship with a Superhero during my 50 plus years of life! This Superhero only comes in second place to the Ultimate Hero, who is my Lord and Savior Jesus Christ. The Superhero I speak of is my earthly father, Bernard Hamilton (aka Pop)! Pop has provided me with a guide on how to "be consistent". I've learned from him that there are three basic areas, or principles, that we should all be consistent in. Those principles are, to "be consistent with yourself", to "be consistent with others", and to "be consistent in your personal relationship with God".

As a boy growing up in the house with my pop, he helped me to understand that having a father to learn from was a gift, because not every boy is fortunate to have a father figure helping them grow into manhood. Pops also knew that tomorrow wasn't promised, so he wanted me to be able to develop into an independent young man, in case something were to happen to him. He taught me the first principle of "being consistent with yourself," and showed me that to be successful in this world, you must first start with yourself. You must make up your mind that you're going to do those things necessary to help you learn, grow, and improve daily. Through my father's guidance, I developed a pattern of being a top student in school. I stayed active through sports and academic events. I always ate healthy meals. Well…. not always (sometimes I had a little junk food mixed in…LOL). I also stayed involved with as many people as I could. Once I got into the work force, I knew that to keep a steady job and move up in the company, I had to be consistent in my work and improving each and every day. This is one reason I've been fortunate to work for the same company for over 27 years. Staying consistent in all these areas mentioned, has helped me stay on the road of success as a black man in this country!

The second principle of being "consistent with others", will have a huge impact in the outcome of your life! I can recall how consistent pops was in caring and providing for his family. He and my mother worked as a team to take care of my younger sister and me. We never experienced being without what we needed. Pops did everything he could to demonstrate his love for his family, by working hard with the same job for over 33 years before he retired. He gave me a great example on how to treat a wife (my mom) and love a daughter (my sister). He was firm and he disciplined me when he had to, but he always followed the discipline with an explanation and love. Pops behavior with his family also carried over to others who he encountered. He consistently treated other family members, friends and co-workers with the same respect and caring ways. If you're not as fortunate to have a father to help raise you, don't allow that to stop you from growing and becoming the man you should be. One day you may become a father, and you can follow those same principles with your own children.

The third, and probably most important principle, which ties the other two together, is being consistent in your personal relationship with our Father God! If you believe in the Creator of the world, and the fact that he created you, and has provided for you all that you need, then you should do all you can to establish and keep a deep relationship with Him. Deepening this relationship requires that we develop a routine of daily devotion, through prayer, and filling our hearts and minds with Godly values, by reading the scriptures and other spiritual guided material. There are over 90 plus scriptures in the bible that talk about being consistent. One of my favorite scriptures is **Proverbs 3:6, which says "In all your ways acknowledge him (God), and he shall direct your path."**

My pops demonstrated to me a consistent walk with God, and that is the very reason why he has been so blessed, which has also been a blessing for me! I've learned from him that the only way I can be successful with my goals and challenges in life is to maintain that consistent relationship with the Father! If you do that, he will open doors for you and guide you in the way you should go.

As I conclude, I must admit that I could never thank my Pops enough for the wonderful example of being consistent! As a boy growing into manhood, there are important traits you must develop to make a positive impact in society. Being consistent is an important part of who you are as a man.

CALL TO ACTION:

Remember to develop the three essential principles of being consistent with yourself, consistent with others, and most importantly consistent with God. Doing this will guide your path to a successful life of manhood!

NOTES

SUCCESS IS IN THE PROCESS

By: Joel Crocker

Credentialed Trainer

The word success is interesting because it is used often but it has a different meaning for everyone. Many people will attach success to having financial wealth (having a lot of money), setting personal goals, and achieving them, and/or making a large impact on the world while also pleasing others. While others tend to define their success based off what their peers are accomplishing. (DON'T!) I'm not going to try to convince you of which one of these ideas is the right or wrong way to determine success, but they each have pros and cons.

As a growing young person, it is going to be up to you to self-reflect and understand, what **you** want to achieve and how **you** want people to see **you**. Notice that the emphasis is on you because these are questions you must explore and figure out for yourself. Certainly, others can help you in this process and the answers may change, but you must hold yourself accountable and responsible for your actions. As you continue to mature, you will realize there is only one thing you can control, and that is your actions. So, I'm going to ask you to begin evaluating and managing your actions towards people, situations, and time. Time is very critical because you only get 24 hours each day. If you waste your time on negativity, hate, or unproductive behavior you reduce your available energy and resources for something better.

The following is your process for success:

1. Success is in the process of learning what interests you and what you do well. Take your skill, sharpen it, and become the best.

2. Success is in the process of managing your daily actions. Whatever actions you are truly committed to will dominate your time.

3. Success is in the process of identifying areas where you need help. No one accomplishes anything by themselves. Find someone who has greater experience than yourself or friends.

4. Success is in the process of viewing disappointment and setbacks as chances to regroup and modify your plan. There are no mistakes, only discoveries. Sometimes you learn more when things don't go as expected as opposed to when they go as planned.

5. Success is in the process of a lifetime of learning and growing. The only constant in life is change so be mentally ready to control your reactions.

You are unique and special! Share your gifts with the world and as you strive for your success help others along the way to reach their success.

CALL TO ACTION:

1. Make a list of things that are important to you.

2. Schedule activities that are important to you to ensure they happen.

3. Identify one activity which you need help from someone else and find someone to assist.

NOTES

SEIZE YOUR DESTINY

By: Charles Teddington, D.R.E.

Minister

The wise man King Solomon said, "A man's gift makes room for him, and bringeth him before great men" (Proverbs 8:16 KJV). God has given you these unique abilities to help you find your way in life. He wants you to succeed in the roles He planned for you. This divine gift can even open doors that were once closed. So, it's important to understand that developing your talents is a big deal because it can bring good things into your life.

However, one must be mindful that in life there are hazards and pitfalls awaiting you to dissuade, discourage, or simply to test your tenacity and stick-to-itiveness in the face of adversity and opposition. When confronted with such, expect to do better than the world imagines of you; expect to live in a bigger and better world than the one that you inherited. Emeritus Harvard Professor Charles Vert Willie cautioned, "By idolizing those whom we honor, we do a disservice both to them and to ourselves.... we fail to recognize that we could go and do likewise."

Perhaps you are familiar with former National Basketball Association (NBA) Allstar Gilbert Arenas. He recently shared on "The No Chill Podcast" an incident that occurred in 2003 between NBA Hall of Famer Michael Jordan and the late NBA great Kobe Bryant, soon to be inducted into the NBA Hall of Fame. Arenas asserted that following a post-game Wizards victory against the Los Angeles Lakers in Washington D.C., Jordan said to Kobe, "You can put the shoes on, but you will never fill them. You're never going to fill these shoes."

(link: https://www.youtube.com/watch?v=hQCp3Nhsxl0)

Arenas stated that following the aftermath of the Jordan incident, Bryant did not speak to his Laker's teammates for an entire two-week period leading up to the team's rematch with the Wizards. Going into that game, Bryant had already become a three-time NBA champion in his own right at just 24 years old. However, Jordan's remark may have unintentionally become the fuel that Bryant internalized to spark a flame resulting in a peak performance in their rematch that would be an accomplishment for the record books. To say that Kobe idolized Jordan is an understatement. All one must do is watch the similarity of how Kobe styled his gameplay after Michael Jordan's. The resemblance and imitation of it is undeniable. Kobe indeed looked up to Jordan as a great basketball player. However, he never failed to recognize and believe that he too could go and do likewise in his own greatness. When it was time for the Wizards rematch in Los Angeles, Kobe dished out 42 points against Jordan and the Wizards in the first half of the game. Kobe put on a show, scoring 55 points in what would stand as his highest scoring total ever against the Washington Wizards.

One of the most challenging realizations for many males of the African American group, is growing up in an America with a persistent mindset of lowering one's goals in the pathway of mediocrity. The world we live in for so many often results in pawned hopes and shattered dreams. You must dream big, and persistently refuse to allow your dreams to be smaller than those of any fellow American. American professional tennis player Arthur Ashe, who just happens to be of African American descent, was the first and the only African American man ever to win the singles title at Wimbledon, the US Open, and the Australian Open. He was a man that refused to be labeled and limited by the complexion of his skin or by the group of people he identified with. He once expressed his view of human achievement and possibility, saying, "My potential is more than can be expressed within the bounds of my race or ethnic identity." I believe he was speaking for all people, everywhere.

When I was a young boy, I heard on more than one occasion the remark that, "I would never amount to much." If you too have heard that stated about you, refuse to believe it and do not internalize the negative forecast that another is trying to sow into your destiny, no matter who they are relationally to you in life. Sometimes all one has is the hope for a better tomorrow and a brighter day to carry them through. As you dream of such, dream big because you are in the preparation phase of life, and you will soon be activating your energy to be a productive contributor to the world. A word of caution, please refuse to be disheartened if there is no offering words of encouragement or support (whether family members or close friends), especially from those who have not been successful in accomplishing much in their own life pursuits. Be discriminative about whom you share your dreams and failures with. People lacking in personal achievement often are incapable of seeing another's potential. And if they do, it is even more of a rarity that they willingly nurture seeds of success into others because they have not obtained it for themselves.

Your self-image, the way you see yourself and think of yourself, rather than your self-esteem, is truly what determines the altitude of your success in life. The word of God states it this way, "For as he thinketh in his heart, so is he" (Proverbs 23:7 KJV). If you can see the invisible, you can absolutely achieve the impossible. The biblical writer of Hebrews put it this way: "Now faith is the assurance of things hoped for, the conviction of things not seen" **(Hebrews 11:1 NASB).** If you want to powerfully transform your self-image and begin to see yourself the way that God sees you. As a son of destiny. the Bible, which is the word of God, is the most powerful and reliable source for you because, if believed and obeyed, it contains the words resulting in eternal life. Man was created in the image of God. This means that man has attributes and characteristics that are in similitude to God. Yet, man's traits are finite in his essence whereas God's nature and essence is perfect, unlimited, and infinite in capacity.

My dearly departed grandfather used to joyfully say to me at the end of our conversations, "In all that you do, make sure to keep God first." I encourage you with these same words.

CALL TO ACTION:

Seek a personal relationship with God through Jesus Christ and his good news message of salvation. God is a rewarder of those who diligently seek after Him. Develop greatness in your character. Your character should be as great, if not greater, than your giftedness. Each day that you awaken and before retiring to bed, give God His worthy praise and thanksgiving. Then repeat these powerful words of the apostle Paul: "I can do all things through Christ which strengtheneth me" (Philippians 4:13 KJV). Speak these divine words aloud in the mirror three times daily, and within the first five (5) days you will begin a new journey of achieving. A new power of belief and bravery will become alive inside of you. Aim to be a success and not another statistic.

Your destiny awaits you. Be courageous and dare to make history!

NOTES

GOLD MEDALS: HOW TO STAY IN THE RACE SO YOU CAN WIN THE RACE

By: Jalen Christopher

College Student

So many times, we get goal setting backwards. We set a goal, we point out why it is good to hit the goal and then we set up a system to reach the goal. You might ask, what is backwards about this approach, it completely avoids what made it so that the goal was not reached in the first place. When someone's habits are taking them in one direction the first step should be to steadily change their habits in a way that is long lasting and sustainable. You hear in every weight loss commercial that the person tried multiple weight loss programs but none of them worked except for the one they are promoting. This is because they have slowly changed their behavioral habits to match their goal. Today I will focus on the less talked about side of goal setting. How to stay on track to reach your goal by making simple changes in your life, making measurable changes, and making sustainable changes, so that once the goal is hit, it is easily replicable.

Keep it simple stupid (K.I.S.S. method) Setting your goal should be like climbing Mount Everest, one step at a time. No man can climb Mount Everest in a full sprint. They do it one step at a time. Reaching your goal should not be done "full sprint" it should be done with simple, easy, and manageable steps that you could do with ease. If you want to become a better reader, read 2 minutes a day and build up. If you want to run a marathon and walk for 2 minutes and build up. If you want to lose weight, have one healthy meal a week and build up. If when you make the goal, you don't say, "Even I can do that!" Then it is not easy enough. The point is to make this goal as attainable as possible.

Once the goal is reached, the next step is to measure growth. This means that you need to have measurable goals that can be objectively critiqued. So, the person that was once reading 2 minutes a day on day 1 is now reading 5 minutes a day on day 6. The person that was trying to run a marathon and walking for 2 minutes on day 1 is walking for 5 minutes on day 3. The person that was losing weight and eating one healthy meal a week by week 1 is now eating 2 healthy meals a week by week 6. The point of this system is not to set deadlines for yourself, but to allow your behavior to build consistent and growing habits. Once the goal is reached, and the growth is measurable, the final step is to maintain it.

What is the benefit of reaching a goal if you have a problem maintaining it. It serves no purpose to reach your goal, feel good, and then revert into your old habits. For example, becoming debt free and then getting into debt a year later Staying debt free allows you to have freedom and enjoy life. So, if you are trying to be a better reader and you went from reading 2 minutes a day to reading 10 minutes a day but if you try 11 minutes you fall off, then stay at 10 minutes until you can. If walking for 30 minutes a day is your max, stay at 30 minutes until you can do 31. If you cannot eat more than 4 healthy meals a week without going on an ice cream binge, stay at 4 healthy meals until you can move your way up to 5. When the goal is attainable it is easily maintained and sustained. You have just set yourself up for climbing your Mount Ever est.

What this boils down to is a negotiation between your present self and your future self. Your future self wants you to be the best version of yourself, and your present self wants to enjoy their life right now. If the two can find a compromise, then everyone can be happy. Set an easily attainable goal like taking 10 steps a day to climb your Mount Everest, make sure this goal is measurable at 10 steps and give room for it to grow to 11. Sticking to the goal keeps it sustained, you are always moving forward towards the top. These three steps repeated, day in and day out, will allow you to reach the top. Not only will you reach your Mount Everest, but you will live on Mount Everest, and as someone who has followed this process, the view from up here is nice.

CALL TO ACTION:

Challenge: Look in your life and find something worth attaining. Start this process by picking your long-term goal, then the short-term goal. Make sure they can easily be attained. Make sure it is measurable and has room to grow. Finally, keep up with it, and if it is too much, take it down a notch.

NOTES

GRATEFUL TO BE HAPPY

By: Butch Chelliah, CEO of BizConnect360.com

I was 16 years old and filled with enough teenage drama to feel like nobody else in the world would ever understand what I was going through. You know the feeling, I'm quite confident that most, if not all of you have experienced it.

I was raised within a faith-filled environment and found myself sitting in church quite often. I would go almost daily when time allowed. I don't exactly know why I went or what I did there but, on many occasions, I would find myself sitting by myself in the quiet of the afternoon when nobody was around.

I was exiting the church one afternoon when I was met by a retired pastor. He was French and spoke with a deep accent. He asked how I was doing as he had seen me sitting in church by myself for quite a while. I replied that I was doing well, which was the standard reply when asked the question by an adult. No grown up was really interested in what I had to say, or so I thought.

He didn't press for more information but started to share a thought with me. He asked if I would try a technique if he would recommend one. He was well liked in the community and had been the pastor for over 40 years. I knew of him but did not know him personally. He for sure didn't know me. I was a little taken aback when he asked the question but remained polite and agreed to engage.

He said, "Every night, as you lie on your pillow, I want you to take a few minutes and reflect on any good moments you experienced during that day. It could be a funny joke you heard, running into an old friend, somebody sharing a happy memory with you, receiving a gift from someone, giving somebody else a gift, essentially any good news or event for that day, that made you smile, or feel loved. I want you to create a list of 10 moments each day. Can you do that?" I thought it was corny as he said it, but I nodded in compliance. He saw through me instantly and said, "I know you think it's cheesy, but would you give it a try?" I promised I would at least try.

It would turn out to be one of the toughest exercises I would attempt. 16-year-olds prefer to be bitter and angry at the world. It was also a challenge to replay moments of each day to identify the moments that would be considered "Happy". 10 Moments? Are there 10 Happy Moments to count? *I was a less privileged minority kid growing up with not much feeling of hope* but still I tried. It took a few days before I could find 10 Happy Moments in my day. It's not that there weren't many happy moments. I was just not skilled in looking for them as a reflection. A few weeks into it, I was hooked. I went to bed happy each night and felt encouraged for more goodness to come the next day. My demeanor was changing each day and I was beginning to like myself for the first time.

Here's a thought, You Can't be Grateful and Unhappy at the Same Time!

I hoped to run into this pastor again to share my progress with him. I learned that he passed away and was dealing with advanced cancer during the time he stopped to speak with me. He didn't share any of that but just spoke of encouragement and hope that day we met. What a testimony of a strategy that works. He lived each day retiring with 10 Happy Thoughts that blessed him each day. I am grateful for the encounter. It's often on my list of 10 Happy Moments that I still draw from things like it happened today.

I must admit that I haven't always performed this exercise each night. Mostly, I forget when I have great, fun, and love-filled days. However, there are many days mixed in with those that are less than inspiring. Days when I don't feel as loved, as fortunate or as rewarded. Days when I didn't love as hard as I should have, been as kind to others as I could have and perhaps less than generous. It is these days that I dig deep to through this exercise. And sometimes, I must dig deep to not be the Grand Marshall of my own pity party.

I have experienced great heartbreaks, huge failures, and massive disappointments in my life. I'm sure that most people can relate to something similar. I am also not suggesting that this was an easy exercise to overcome. I just know that without the gift of this challenge by the pastor who stopped me many years ago, I wouldn't have survived as well as I did, and I wouldn't have been able to help the people who were counting on me along the way to help them get through life.

I have been blessed and fortunate to positively affect many people's lives. Some I get to help emotionally, others I get to help financially. Either way, you can't be of service to others, if you're a wreck yourself. I like that there's an opportunity presented to me each day to be grateful so I can avoid being unhappy.

CALL TO ACTION:

Here's the challenge for you.

1. Decide that we could all use some help along the way.

2. Recognize that there will be Unhappy Days

3. Accept the things you cannot Change and have Courage to change the things you Can.

4. Love Others

5. Love Yourself

I invite you to join me every day for this exercise. You can reach out to me at

www.ButchChelliah.com if you need an exercise partner.

I have learned that even on the darkest days, the loneliest of times and the scariest of moments, there are 10 Happy Moments that we can draw from that happens every day.

NOTES

Congratulations on making it through this guide!!

The Gentlemen that contributed to this book took time out of the hustle and bustle of their lives to impart some of their knowledge and experiences to help you along your journey. It is our greatest aspiration that you have found this helpful, relatable, inspirational, and downright on point with helping you navigate through this sometimes-tumultuous life.

This week, I want you to reflect on all the notes you took throughout the past 52 weeks. Consider the growth, the ah-ha moments, the dang, I wish I had known that a year ago episodes.

You have come a long way and please know; this is just the beginning. This book is just a taste of what life is going to throw at you. You will be better prepared but there is so much more to learn, to experience, to contemplate.

Never stop growing, never stop learning, never stop challenging yourselves to push harder every day.

When it gets tough, when you feel like you just can't take another breath without wanting to give up or give in, read from this book. Call on someone you know to give you sound advice. God is the ultimate listener. He will guide you through the pits of life.

There will be great times too. Enjoy them, don't let anyone steal your joy. Cherish those times, embrace, and understand what it took to get to those moments. Celebrate the small wins as well as the monumental ones.

If you haven't noticed by now, you will. Life is like a rollercoaster, fun times, challenging times, highs, lows, and a whole lot of screaming. Stay the course, keep your hand in God's hand and He will see you through.

We love you. We are proud of you. We believe in you and what you're capable of becoming.

"The moment you recognize what truly drives you to push harder than anything you've ever done is the day you begin to Run Your Dreams"

-Ernie D. Seay, Editor

Owner of Run Your Dreams

www.ingramcontent.com/pod-product-compliance
Lightning Source LLC
Chambersburg PA
CBHW071401150726

48000CB00001B/115